SPECTRUM®

Test Prep

Grade 7

Published by Spectrum®
An imprint of Carson-Dellosa Publishing LLC
Greensboro, North Carolina

Spectrum®
An imprint of Carson-Dellosa Publishing LLC
P.O. Box 35665
Greensboro, NC 27425 USA

ISBN 978-1-4838-1374-5

01-349147811

Table of Contents

What's Inside?

Spectrum Test Prep is designed to help you and your seventh grader prepare and plan for success on standardized tests.

Strategies

This workbook is structured around strategies. A strategy is a careful plan or method for achieving a particular goal, such as succeeding on a test. Strategies can be broad general strategies about a test as a whole or a category of skills. Strategies can also be specific, providing step-by-step instructions on how to tackle a problem or offering guidelines on how to answer a question about a story. Learning how to apply a strategy gives test-takers a plan for how to approach a test as a whole and how to answer questions.

This workbook offers a set of broader strategies and very specific strategies. General test-taking strategies apply to all tests, and should be used to help prepare for the test. Specific strategies for English Language Arts and Mathematics tests are divided into larger categories of skills students will encounter, such as reading literature or performing calculations. On each practice page, you will find even more specific strategies that apply to the skills.

Test Tips

Test Tips are included throughout the practice page. While strategies offer a plan for answering test items, Test Tips offer ideas for how to apply each strategy or how to approach a type of question. There are Test Tips that apply to all tests and Test Tips for English Language Arts and Mathematics tests.

Practice Pages

The workbook is divided into two sections, English Language Arts and Mathematics. Each section has practice activities that have questions similar to those that will appear on standardized tests. Also included are strategies and Test Tips to guide students. Students should use a pencil to complete these activities.

Strategy Review Pages

Strategy review pages give your student an opportunity to review and practice important strategies in each content area. These strategies cover the important skills students will encounter on tests in English Language Arts and Mathematics.

Answer Key

Answers for all of the practice pages and strategy review pages are found in an answer key at the end of the book.

Test-Taking Strategies

Being prepared is key to doing your best on test day. Read the tips below to help you prepare for tests.

In the days before the test...

- Keep up on your reading, worksheets, and assignments. Completing all your assigned work will help you be better prepared for the test.

- Don't wait until right before the test to review materials. Create a study schedule for the best result. That way, you can study a bit at a time and not all at once.

- Take advantage of sample items and practice tests. Complete these to practice for your test. If you run into concepts or skills that are new, ask a teacher or other adult

The night before the test...

- Don't try to study everything all over again the night before. If you've been studying in the days before the test, all you need to do the night before is a light review of your notes. Remind yourself of the key ideas and practice a few skills, but don't study late into the night.

- Make sure you have all the materials you will need for the test, such as pencils, paper, or a calculator. Check with your teacher to make sure you know what tools to bring. Having everything ready the night before will make the morning less stressful.

- Get a good night's sleep the night before the test. If you are well rested, you will be more alert and able to do your best.

On the day of the test...

- Don't skip breakfast. If you are hungry, you won't be thinking about the test. You'll be thinking about lunch.

- Make sure you have at least two sharpened pencils with you and any other tools needed.

- Read all directions carefully. Make sure you understand how you are supposed to answer each question.

- For multiple choice questions, read all the possible answers before choosing one. If you know that some answers are wrong, cross them off. Even if you have to guess, this will eliminate some wrong answers.

- Once you choose or write an answer, double check it by reading the question again. Confirm that your answer is correct.

- Answer every part of a question. If a question asks you to show your work or to explain how you arrived at an answer, make sure you include that information.

- If you are stuck on a question, or are unsure, mark it lightly with a pencil and move on. If you have time, you can come back. This is especially true on a timed test.

- Breathe! Remind yourself that you've prepared for the test and that you will do your best!

Strategies for English Language Arts Tests

Use details from the text to make inferences, understand theme, and draw out meaning.
Writers carefully choose details to include in their writing. Every detail matters. Each one is included for a purpose. As you read stories, look for details that help you understand what the writer is saying about characters, events, and the overall meaning, or theme. As you read passages, look for details that give reasons that support any opinions or facts the writer shares, as well as the central or main idea.

Identify literary or structural elements and use them to understand the meaning of a text.
Writers use literary elements such as figurative language to bring more meaning to their writing. They choose a structure that reflects their purpose for writing. Read carefully for ways that these elements help you understand the meaning of a story, poem, or passage.

Look carefully at visuals, such as illustrations, diagrams, or graphs, to see how they connect to the text.
Visuals are always related to the text. It is up to readers to figure out the connection. Does the visual explain something that is difficult to say in words? Does it add detail? As you read stories and passages, look carefully at visuals to see what information they provide.

Reread texts to make comparisons, draw conclusions, or support inferences.
Every reader has his or her own ideas about a text. If you are asked to draw a conclusion about what the writer means or thinks, however, you need to rely on details in the text, not your own opinions. When you have drawn a conclusion or made an inference, reread the text to make sure you can support it with facts, examples, and other information from the text.

Use word clues in a text to identify its structure, to see how ideas in a text are related, and to clarify word meanings.
Some words are signals that a text has a particular structure. For example, the words *cause* and *because* often signal a cause-and-effect structure. You may also be able to use words as clues to the meaning of unfamiliar words.

When writing, use details to support, explain, or clarify your main ideas.
In persuasive and informational writing, it is important to make sure you support and explain each main idea with details. Facts, examples, and logical reasoning can all be used to make your main ideas strong and clear.

Use an outline to plan your writing.
Prewriting activities, such as outlining, can make writing clear and make your ideas easy to understand. A simple outline that lists main ideas or claims followed by their supporting details is enough to make your writing flow more easily.

Use transitions to show how ideas are related.
As you write, use transitions to help your reader follow your train of thought. You may know how your ideas are related, but readers need a little extra help! For example, the transition *As a result* shows that you are explaining a cause and an effect. The transitions *Next* and *Finally* help readers see that you are explaining a process or events that happen in a certain order.

Revise to make sure your writing is clear and makes sense. Then, edit to fix errors.
After you finish your draft, you may have time to revise and edit. First, revise to make sure your words say what you wanted them to say. Then, check spelling, capitalization, punctuation, and grammar to catch and fix errors.

English Language Arts

Cite Text Evidence to Support Analysis
Reading: Literature

DIRECTIONS: Read the poem. Then, answer the questions using details from the poem.

The Little Black-Eyed Rebel *by Will Carleton*

A boy drove into the city, his wagon loaded down
With food to feed the people of the British-governed town;
And the little black-eyed rebel, so innocent and sly,
Was watching for his coming from the corner of her eye. . . .

He drove up to the market, he waited in the line;
His apples and potatoes were fresh and fair and fine;
But long and long he waited, and no one came to buy,
Save the black-eyed rebel, watching from the corner of her eye.

"Now who will buy my apples?" he shouted, long and loud;
And "Who wants my potatoes?" he repeated to the crowd;
But from all the people round him came no word of reply,
Save the black-eyed rebel, answering from the corner of her eye.

For she knew that 'neath the lining of the coat he wore that day,
Were long letters from the husbands and the fathers far away,
Who were fighting for the freedom that they meant to gain or die;
And a tear like silver glistened in the corner of her eye.

But the treasures—how to get them? crept the questions through her mind,
Since keen enemies were watching for what prizes they might find;
And she paused a while and pondered, with a pretty little sigh;
Then resolve crept through her features, and a shrewdness fired her eye.

So she resolutely walked up to the wagon old and red;
"May I have a dozen apples for a kiss?" she sweetly said:
And the brown face flushed to scarlet; for the boy was somewhat shy,
And he saw her laughing at him from the corner of her eye. . . .

Clinging round his brawny neck, she clasped her fingers white and small,
And then whispered, "Quick! the letters! thrust them underneath my shawl!
Carry back again *this* package, and be sure that you are spry!"
And she sweetly smiled upon him from the corner of her eye. . . .

With the news of loved ones absent to the dear friends they would greet,
Searching them who hungered for them, swift she glided through the street.
"There is nothing worth the doing that it does not pay to try,"
Thought the little black-eyed rebel, with a twinkle in her eye.

English Language Arts

Cite Text Evidence to Support Analysis
Reading: Literature

Strategy When reading, identify details that are clues to the setting, or the time and place in which this poem is set.

Test Tip To identify the setting, look for details about where the little rebel lives and why her relatives are fighting.

1. **PART A: When does the action in this poem take place?**

   (A) during the French and Indian Wars

   (B) during the American Revolution

   (C) during Shays' Rebellion

   (D) during the War of 1812

   Part B: Which lines from the poem best support your answer to Part A? Choose three answers.

   (A) ". . . With food to feed the people of the British-governed town;"

   (B) "His apples and potatoes were fresh and fair and fine;"

   (C) ". . . Who were fighting for the freedom that they meant to gain or die;"

   (D) "But the treasures—how to get them?"

   (E) " 'May I have a dozen apples for a kiss?' "

   (F) "...Thought the little black-eyed rebel with a twinkle in her eye."

2. **What effect does the poet create by ending each stanza with "her eye"?**

   _____

   _____

   _____

   _____

3. **Which detail from the poem helps to clarify the meaning of *clinging*?**

   (A) The girl asks for a kiss.

   (B) The boy was somewhat shy.

   (C) The girl clasped her fingers.

   (D) The boy's face flushed scarlet.

4. **Which line shows how the girl feels in stanza 4?**

   _____

   _____

   Write how you know. Why does she feel that way?

   _____

   _____

5. **What problem does the little black-eyed rebel need to solve? Cite at least one line from the poem to support your answer.**

   _____

   _____

   _____

   _____

   _____

   _____

   _____

English Language Arts

Determine Theme
Reading: Literature

DIRECTIONS: Read the story. Then, answer the questions.

Growing Pains

"I never should have tried out for the team," grumbled Chris, slumping to the floor. "When we ran drills today, I tripped over my own feet—*twice*."

"You're just having a growth spurt," replied his grandmother. "Once you're used to your new body, you'll hardly remember how awkward you felt growing into it."

"Yeah, right," said Chris with a skeptical expression.

"Listen," his grandmother said. "I have a story to tell you."

"Not another story," Chris groaned, but he settled himself to listen.

"An ant running about in search of food came across a chrysalis," said his grandmother as she settled into her storytelling rhythm.

"The ant stopped dashing about to look more closely at the lumpy casing hanging from a twig. Its hard, shiny surface was turning transparent in places, allowing a brightly colored pattern to show through. The ant could not see enough of the pattern to guess what kind of creature lived inside the shell.

" 'Poor creature,' said the ant. 'I can run wherever I want, exploring the smallest flower or the tallest tree. You can only lie in your shell. We ants are free to move about.'

"The chrysalis heard all this, but did not reply. A few days later, when the ant passed that way again, he saw that the shell was empty. As he stopped to wonder what had become of the creature inside, he felt himself overshadowed by the gorgeous wings of a butterfly.

" 'You pitied me,' said the butterfly floating overhead, 'and took pride in your freedom to move about wherever you please. Boast now of your powers to run and climb—as long as you can get me to listen.'

" 'So saying, the butterfly soared into the air. The ant watched in amazement as the butterfly was borne along on the summer breeze, out of his sight forever.'"

English Language Arts

Determine Theme
Reading: Literature

Strategy | Focus on details related to what a character learns about life or how the character faces a problem in order to identify the theme of a story.

Test Tip | To identify theme in this story, ask: *What lesson does Chris need to learn to solve his problem?*

1. What is the problem that Chris faces?

_____

_____

_____

2. What do the words "slumping to the floor" tell you about Chris?

Ⓐ He is discouraged.

Ⓑ He is furious.

Ⓒ He is proud.

Ⓓ He is thrilled.

Write how you know.

_____

_____

_____

3. Why does Chris' grandmother insist on telling him a story?

Ⓐ to help him accept his limitations

Ⓑ to show him how to become a better athlete

Ⓒ to encourage him to have patience with himself

Ⓓ to teach him to treat others with more respect

Write how you know.

_____

_____

_____

_____

4. Write the sentence that shows Chris doesn't believe he will get used to his new body as his grandmother says.

_____

_____

_____

_____

5. Which character in the fable Chris' grandmother tells is most like Chris? Explain, using details from the story.

_____

_____

_____

_____

_____

_____

English Language Arts

Determine Theme
Reading: Literature

Strategy Combine the dialogue and words that tell what a character thinks or does to get a complete understanding of a character. Use that understanding to identify theme.

6. **Which sentence below would make the best moral for the fable Chris' grandmother told?**

   (A) Beauty is only skin deep.

   (B) Curiosity will lead you to many unexpected discoveries.

   (C) Boast as much as you like as long as you can back up what you say.

   (D) If you judge someone only by appearances, you will often be wrong.

7. **What method does the author use to develop the theme of this story?**

   (A) A character tells a story within a story.

   (B) Chris' grandmother explains cause-and-effect.

   (C) A moral at the end of the fable sums up the lesson.

   (D) The narrator moves between the present and the past.

   Write how you know.

   _____

   _____

   _____

   _____

8. **What does Chris' grandmother want him to learn from the story of the chrysalis? Explain.**

   _____

   _____

   _____

   _____

   _____

   _____

   _____

9. **Will Chris' grandmother help Chris by telling the story? Explain your answer.**

   _____

   _____

   _____

   _____

   _____

   _____

   _____

10. **If Chris' grandmother is right, how will Chris play in future practices? Explain your answer.**

   _____

   _____

   _____

   _____

   _____

   _____

   _____

Test Tip

Even when a question does not ask specifically for details from a story or passage, identify details and include them in your answer. The details support your answer.

English Language Arts
Analyze Interaction of Story Elements
Reading: Literature

DIRECTIONS: Read the story. Then, answer the questions.

A New Tepee

Fingers of frost tickled Little Deer's feet. It was a chilly autumn morning, but there was no time to snuggle beneath her buffalo skins. It was going to be a busy day, helping her mother to finish the cover for their family's new tepee.

Little Deer slid her tunic over her head and fastened her moccasins. Wrapping herself in another skin, she walked outside to survey what they had done so far. The tepee cover was beautiful and nearly complete. The vast semicircle was spread across the ground, a patchwork in various shades of brown. After her father and brothers had killed the buffalo, she and her mother had carefully cured and prepared the skins, stretching them and scraping them until they were buttery soft. Then, with needles made from bone and thread made from animal sinew, they had sewn the hides together to form a huge canvas nearly thirty feet across.

Little Deer remembered the day she had learned to make needles. She had watched as her mother had cut grooves into dried leg bones with a sharp flint stone. As usual, she used the flint to break off splinters. Then, for the first time, she handed a splinter to Little Deer. Imitating her mother, Little Deer rubbed the splinter with a piece of granite to smooth the sharp edges. The work went slowly, so Little Deer rubbed harder and harder until the bone fragment broke. Her mother said nothing but gave her another piece of bone. Then, she put her hands over Little Deer's to show her how much pressure to use. When the fragment finally had a smooth, sharp point, her mother showed her how to use the flint to cut a hole for the thread.

"You have learned much today, Little Deer," her mother had said. "Now you know how to turn a leg bone into a needle." Before Little Deer could feel too proud, her mother asked teasingly, "And did you learn something about patience, too?"

Little Deer smiled at the memory. Today they would at long last finish the cover. Then, it would be ready to mount on the lodge poles. Little Deer's father had traded with another tribe for fourteen tall, wooden poles. They would stack the poles together in a cone shape, lashing them together with more rope made from animal sinews. Then, they would carefully stretch the cover over the poles, forming a snug, watertight home.

Little Deer smiled in anticipation. She could just imagine the cozy glow of the fire through the tepee walls at night.

English Language Arts

Analyze Interaction of Story Elements
Reading: Literature

Strategy | To understand how story elements interact, ask yourself how the setting, characters, and events are all connected.

Test Tip | To identify how the characters and the setting interact in "A New Tepee," ask how this story would be different if the characters lived in the same time and place as you.

1. **Write details from the first paragraph that tell you about the setting of the story.**

   _____

   _____

   _____

2. **Why did Little Deer have "no time to snuggle beneath her buffalo skins"?**

   (A) She was going hunting with her brothers.

   (B) She was mounting the lodge poles.

   (C) She was making needles out of bone.

   (D) She was sewing the cover of the tepee.

   Write how you know.

   _____

   _____

   _____

3. **PART A: Why does Little Deer's family need a new tepee?**

   (A) to have a more beautiful tepee

   (B) for protection from enemies

   (C) to keep them warm in cold weather

   (D) to replace one that does not have a cover

   PART B: Write details from the story that you used to help you answer Part A.

   _____

   _____

   _____

4. **How does Little Deer's family use natural resources to survive on the Great Plains? Use at least three details from the story to support your answer.**

   _____

   _____

   _____

   _____

   _____

   _____

   _____

   _____

English Language Arts

Analyze Interaction of Story Elements
Reading: Literature

Strategy To determine how the characters respond to their environment in "A New Tepee," identify what things are important to them.

5. Why does Little Deer's mother think her daughter needs to learn patience?

(A) Little Deer tends to act first and think later.

(B) The needle Little Deer breaks cannot easily be replaced.

(C) Little Deer's mother takes the time needed to do things correctly.

(D) The things Little Deer's family needs require a great deal of time to make.

Write how you know.

_____

_____

_____

6. How does Little Deer's mother try to keep her daughter from becoming too proud?

(A) She tells Little Deer she is now ready for more difficult challenges.

(B) She insists that Little Deer keep working until she makes the needle correctly.

(C) She gently reminds Little Deer that she needs to take her time when making needles.

(D) She tells Little Deer that she has learned something, but she still has much more to learn.

7. What might you learn about Native American values from the way the family interacts with the environment and with each other?

_____

_____

_____

_____

_____

_____

_____

_____

_____

_____

_____

_____

_____

_____

_____

_____

_____

_____

_____

_____

_____

_____

_____

_____

English Language Arts

Interpret Figurative Language and Poetic Elements
Reading: Literature

DIRECTIONS: Read the poem.

The Railway Train *by Emily Dickinson*

I   I like to see it lap the miles,
And lick the valleys up,
And stop to feed itself at tanks;
And then, prodigious[1], step

5   Around a pile of mountains,
And, supercilious[2], peer
In shanties, by the sides of roads;
And then a quarry pare

To fit its sides, and crawl between,
10 Complaining all the while
In horrid, hooting stanza;
Then chase itself down hill

And neigh like Boanerges[3];
Then, punctual as a star,
15 Stop—docile[4] and omnipotent[5]—
At its own stable door.

[1] *prodigious*—enormous
[2] *supercilious*—arrogant; acts superior to others
[3] *Boanerges*—a name that means "Son of Thunder"; a loud public speaker
[4] *docile*—obedient, submissive; easy to control
[5] *omnipotent*—all powerful

Strategy
To better understand poems, identify and interpret figurative language.

Test Tip
Similes use a comparison word, such as *like* or *as*. Use these words as clues to identify and interpret similes. Metaphors just compare two unlike things without any word clues.

1. This poem is a metaphor that compares a train to a horse. What words are clues that show the author is comparing the train to a horse?

_____

_____

_____

2. Which line includes a simile?

Ⓐ line 2
Ⓑ line 10
Ⓒ line 12
Ⓓ line 14

Write how you know.

_____

_____

3. Use details from the poem to write a simile comparing a train and a horse.

_____

_____

_____

Interpret Figurative Language and Poetic Elements
Reading: Literature

Strategy | As you read, identify words and phrases that don't seem to have literal meanings. Then, find the meaning that makes sense in the poem.

Test Tip | First, make sure you understand what is happening in the poem by identifying who is speaking and the poem's topic, or what the poem is mainly about. Then, find figurative language and poetic elements that add a deeper meaning.

4. Alliteration is the repetition of the same or similar consonants at the beginnings of nearby words. Identify an example of alliteration in the poem.

_____

_____

_____

_____

5. Reread the first stanza. Write in your own words what the train is doing using details from the poem.

_____

_____

_____

_____

_____

6. The author uses the words *docile* and *omnipotent* together. These words suggest that the train stops at the end of its journey because

Ⓐ the train's engineer is able to make it obey.

Ⓑ it has no ability to act on its own and continue.

Ⓒ it is willing to obey the engineer despite its great strength.

Ⓓ the engineer is giving it a welcome chance to rest after its journey.

7. Which of these words is the best synonym for *supercilious*?

Ⓐ dignified

Ⓑ proud

Ⓒ satisfied

Ⓓ sneering

Write how you know.

_____

_____

_____

_____

8. The word *Boanerges* is an allusion, a type of figurative language which is a way of referring to something without mentioning it directly. How might a train be compared to the name "Son of Thunder" or to a public speaker with a loud voice?

_____

_____

_____

_____

_____

Analyze Structure and Form
Reading: Literature

DIRECTIONS: Read the poem. Then, answer the questions.

Sonnet 43 *by Elizabeth Barrett Browning*

How do I love thee? Let me count the ways.
I love thee to the depth and breadth and height
My soul can reach, when feeling out of sight
For the ends of Being and ideal Grace.
I love thee to the level of every day's
Most quiet need, by sun and candle-light.
I love thee freely, as men strive for Right;
I love thee purely, as they turn from Praise.
I love thee with the passion put to use
In my old griefs, and with my childhood's faith.
I love thee with a love I seemed to lose
With my lost saints,—I love thee with the breath,
Smiles, tears, of all my life!—and, if God choose,
I shall but love thee better after death.

Strategy As you read a poem, identify repetition and rhyme to discover more about the meaning of the poem.

Test Tip Repetition is a way of creating emphasis or importance. What idea is the poet emphasizing in this poem to her husband through the use of repetition?

1. Which describe the poem's structure?

Ⓐ moral and lessons

Ⓑ paragraph and sentences

Ⓒ scenes and dialogue

Ⓓ stanza and rhyming lines

Write how you know.

_____

_____

_____

2. The title of the poem is "Sonnet 43." The word *sonnet* comes from the Italian word *sonetto*, which means "a little sound or song." How is this poem like a little song? Think about rhyme and rhythm.

_____

_____

_____

3. What three words are repeated at the beginning of several lines in this poem?

_____

_____

_____

Analyze Structure and Form
Reading: Literature

Strategy   Identify a poem's rhyme scheme to follow the rhythm intended by the poet.

Test Tip

A rhyme scheme identifies the pattern of lines in a poem that rhyme. The first line is labeled A. Any other lines that end with the same sound as line A are also labeled A. The second line is labeled B, and any lines that end with the same sound are also labeled B. The first stanza of a poem is shown below. It has a rhyme scheme of ABABAB.

She walks in beauty, like the night
Of cloudless climes and starry skies;
And all that's best of dark and bright
Meet in her aspect and her eyes:
Thus mellowed to that tender light
Which heaven to gaudy day denies.

4. How can identifying the rhyme scheme help you understand a poem?

_____

_____

5. If the stanza shown above had 3 lines that ended with the words *rays*, *days*, *stays*, what might the rhyme scheme be?

(A) ABCABCABC

(B) AAABBB

(C) CABCABCAB

(D) ABABAB

Write how you know.

_____

_____

6. In "Sonnet 43" the rhyme scheme is called *iambic pentameter*. Which best shows the rhyme scheme? Remember that all the lines that rhyme are labeled with the same letter.

(A) ABBA ABBA CDC DCD

(B) ABAB ABAB CCC DDD

(C) ABBA ABBA CDC CDC

(D) BBBB AAAA CDC DCD

7. How does the ending of the "Sonnet 43" heighten the effect of the repetition in the earlier lines?

(A) It changes the wording slightly to add variety.

(B) It uses rhyme to reinforce the meaning of the repeated phrase.

(C) It uses the future tense to suggest her love will last for all eternity.

(D) It breaks from the repetitive pattern to introduce a conflicting idea.

8. Why does the poet capitalize words like Grace and Right? Choose the two <u>best</u> answers.

(A) They are proper nouns.

(B) The poet wanted to emphasize them.

(C) Uppercase letters show that they represent ideal qualities.

(D) She made up her own rules for spelling and capitalization.

(E) The rules for capitalization were different when she wrote the poem.

English Language Arts

Identify Point of View
Reading: Literature

DIRECTIONS: Read the passage below. Then, answer the questions.

> According to a Greek myth, Daedalus was a builder who had a son named Icarus. Daedalus solved a problem for Minos, the king of Crete. The king wanted a place to hide a monster, called Minotaur, who was half man and half bull. Daedalus designed the labyrinth, a maze of complicated passages that is very difficult to escape.
>
> Then, Daedalus did something that made Minos very angry, and the king made Daedalus and Icarus prisoners in the labyrinth. One day, Daedalus got an idea as he was watching birds fly. He asked Icarus to gather up all the bird feathers he could find. Then, using the feathers and some wax, Daedalus created two large pairs of wings. Soon, he and Icarus were on their way over the walls of the labyrinth.

Strategy

Look for clues in a story to identify its point of view. The pronouns *I*, *me*, and *we* are clues to first-person point of view. The pronouns *he*, *she*, *him*, and *her* are clues to third-person point of view.

Test Tip

The word *omniscient* means "all-knowing." Something that is *limited* ends at a certain point. So, if the third-person narrator is omniscient, the narrator knows the thoughts of most or all of the characters. If the third-person narrator is limited, the narrator just knows the thoughts of one or a few characters.

1. Which point of view is used in this passage?

(A) first person

(B) second person

(C) third person limited

(D) third person omniscient

Write how you know.

_____

_____

_____

_____

_____

_____

English Language Arts

Identify Point of View
Reading: Literature

DIRECTIONS: Read the next part of the myth, which is told from a different point of view. Then, answer the questions that follow.

As we leave the ground, I hear my father say something like "Do not fly too close to the sun, or your wings will melt." But I do not hear him well over the rush of wind in my ears. I pump my arms harder and faster and then . . . I'm flying! I'm really flying! Each beat of my wings takes me higher, higher, high— Suddenly, I am not moving any more. I notice white feathery pieces floating down to Earth. A feather? My wings! They are melting!

Strategy To identify the point of view, answer these questions: *Who is telling the story? What does he or she know about the characters and events?*

Test Tip Reread the story and focus on words that are clues about who might be telling the story, such as words that tell about a character's age or how they think.

2. **Part A: Whose point of view is the second part of the myth told from?**

   (A) Daedalus

   (B) Icarus

   (C) King Minos

   (D) the Minotaur

   Part B: Which sentence best explains your answer to Part A?

   (A) Icarus speaks for himself, using the pronoun *I*.

   (B) The characters describe sensory details like "white feathery pieces."

   (C) Readers know the exact words Daedalus says to his son.

   (D) The narrator explains what each character is thinking and feeling.

3. **Write words and phrases from the story that helped you identify the point of view.**

   _____

   _____

4. **Which sentence best explains the difference in each narrator's point of view?**

   (A) Icarus knows how to fly higher using the wings Daedalus created.

   (B) Daedalus is overly concerned with the safety of his son.

   (C) Daedalus knows that the wings will melt; Icarus does not.

   (D) Icarus is not concerned with what happens to his father.

   Write how you know.

   _____

   _____

   _____

5. **Why do you think the author chose to tell the story of the flight from a different point of view? Use details from the story to support your answer.**

   _____

   _____

English Language Arts

Compare Fiction and Nonfiction
Reading: Literature

DIRECTIONS: Read the biography of a Civil War drummer boy. Then, answer the questions.

Strategy — Read paired passages individually, and then, reread to focus on comparing them. As you compare fiction and nonfiction, look for differences in point of view, amount of detail, and style.

Drummer Boy and Hero: Orion P. Howe

Orion Perseus Howe became a Union drummer boy at the age of 12. His father was the regimental bandleader for an Illinois infantry unit. Howe served with his father's unit, beating the drum signals that coordinated the soldiers' movements.

During the Battle of Vicksburg, Colonel Malmborg's unit ran dangerously low on ammunition. Howe, one of four volunteers who ran to the rear to deliver the request for more cartridges, was the only runner to get through. An eyewitness reported, "He ran through what seemed a hailstorm of canister and musket-balls." Though wounded, Howe delivered the request for ammunition to General Sherman. He recovered from his injuries and, in all, participated in 14 battles during the war. For his heroism at the Battle of Vicksburg, the drummer boy from Illinois became one of the youngest Americans to earn the Congressional Medal of Honor.

---

1. An author writing about a fictional drummer boy might make up dialogue between the boy and General Sherman. Why does the nonfiction writer use eyewitness testimony instead of dialogue?

_____

_____

_____

_____

_____

2. PART A: Which sentence from the passage describes Howe's heroism during the Battle of Vicksburg?

_____

_____

_____

_____

PART B: Does an eyewitness account hold more weight than a journalist's account? Explain your answer.

_____

_____

_____

3. Which sentence describes Howe's bravery?

(A) "Howe served with his father's unit, beating the drum signals that coordinated the soldiers' movements."

(B) "Orion Perseus Howe became a Union drummer boy at the age of 12."

(C) "During the Battle of Vicksburg, Colonel Malmborg's unit ran dangerously low on ammunition."

(D) "Though wounded, Howe delivered the request for ammunition to General Sherman."

Compare Fiction and Nonfiction
Reading: Literature

DIRECTIONS: The following letter is from a fictional account of a drummer boy in the Civil War. Read the letter. Then, answer the questions.

Strategy As you read paired passages, identify the genre of each passage. Use the features of the genre to understand the kind of information presented and the purpose of the passage.

Test Tip Authors of historical fiction use realistic details to help you get a sense of what life was like for people living at that time. However, other parts of a historical fiction story are not real.

Corydon, Indiana

July the 9th, 1863

Sister Dear:

I am writing this letter in haste before our regiment leaves for Fort Curtis, Arkansas. We saw our first action when General Morgan marched on Corydon. We lined up along the Mauckport road to stop the Confederates' advance and held there until the rebels brought artillery up. When faced with three cannons, we had to leave the battlefield. However, our casualties were limited to four dead and two wounded.

I wanted to reassure you that I am safe and well. When I enlisted, I claimed to be 18, but our commander saw through my pretense and made me a drummer boy. Jeb Bridger is helping me learn the cadences we have to beat. Unfortunately, I had to sound retreat at the Battle of Corydon, but I hope and pray our endeavors meet with greater success in the South.

Your loving brother,

Sam

4. **List at least two similarities between the fictional drummer boy and Orion P. Howe.**

_____

_____

_____

_____

_____

_____

_____

5. **Sam's letter is based on an eyewitness description of the Battle of Corydon. Why do you think fiction writers often research actual events and people?**

_____

_____

_____

_____

_____

_____

English Language Arts

Cite Text Evidence to Support Analysis and Inferences
Reading: Informational Text

DIRECTIONS: Read the passage. Then, answer the questions on the next page.

Caring for Animals
from Ready.gov

If you are like millions of animal owners nationwide, your pet is an important member of your household. Unfortunately, animals are also affected by disaster.

The likelihood that you and your animals will survive an emergency such as a fire, flood, tornado, or terrorist attack depends largely on emergency planning done today. Some of the things you can do to prepare for the unexpected, such as assembling an animal emergency supply kit and developing a pet care buddy system, are the same for any emergency. Whether you decide to stay put in an emergency or evacuate to a safer location, you will need to make plans in advance for your pets. Keep in mind that what's best for you is typically what's best for your animals.

If you evacuate your home, DO NOT LEAVE YOUR PETS BEHIND! Pets most likely cannot survive on their own and if by some remote chance they do, you may not be able to find them when you return.

If you are going to a public shelter, it is important to understand that animals may not be allowed inside. Plan in advance for shelter alternatives that will work for both you and your pets; consider loved ones or friends outside of your immediate area who would be willing to host you and your pets in an emergency.

Make a back-up emergency plan in case you can't care for your animals yourself. Develop a buddy system with neighbors, friends, and relatives to make sure that someone is available to care for or evacuate your pets if you are unable to do so. Be prepared to improvise and use what you have on hand to make it on your own for at least three days, maybe longer.

Cite Text Evidence to Support Analysis and Inferences
Reading: Informational Text

Strategy As you read, identify details that help you analyze and make inferences.

Test Tip Identify the purpose of an informational passage to help you better understand why certain details are included.

1. **Which line from the passage best shares its purpose?**

   (A) "If you are like millions of animal owners nationwide, your pet is an important member of your household."

   (B) "Unfortunately, animals are also affected by disaster."

   (C) "Whether you decide to stay put in an emergency or evacuate to a safer location, you will need to make plans in advance for your pets."

   (D) "If you are going to a public shelter, it is important to understand that animals may not be allowed inside."

2. **Which conclusion can be supported by details from the passage?**

   (A) Pets have simpler needs than people, so you should not worry about them.

   (B) Making an emergency plan for your pets is an important part of responsible pet ownership.

   (C) Shelters do not accept pets because animals may pose a health concern for some people.

   (D) If you are in an emergency situation, neighbors and friends will probably not be available.

3. **Consider this sentence from the passage:**

   "Keep in mind that what's best for you is typically what's best for your animals."

   What does the author mean? What clues in the rest of the paragraph help you understand the types of things you should do for your pet?

   _____

   _____

   _____

   _____

   _____

   _____

   _____

   _____

   _____

   _____

Summarize Using Central Ideas and Key Details
Reading: Informational Text

DIRECTIONS: Read the passage. Then, answer the questions on the next page.

From Kitty Hawk to the Moon

Less than 100 years after Orville and Wilbur Wright's first flight at Kitty Hawk in 1903, humans were flying in space. The first manned space flight occurred in 1961 when Russian cosmonaut Yuri A. Gagarin orbited Earth a single time. In 1963, the first woman cosmonaut, Valentina Tereshkova, orbited the Earth 48 times.

The Space Race: Competition

In 1957, the Soviet Union launched the first satellite to orbit the earth. The launch of Sputnik gave them an early lead in the space race, which they led for many years. In 1965, cosmonaut Aleksey A. Leonov took the first space walk. In 1968, the Russians launched an unmanned spacecraft that orbited the moon.

However, by that time the United States was also racing to be the first to land on the lunar surface. In 1961, President Kennedy promised the United States would reach the moon within 10 years. In 1969, Neil Armstrong took "one small step for [a] man, one giant leap for mankind."

New Frontiers: Cooperation

Today, people continue their quest for space exploration, gathering data from the International Space Station. The success of that venture has encouraged 14 space agencies from around the world to plan additional joint projects to explore our solar system. One goal is that first robots and then humans will someday explore the surface of Mars. In addition, the cooperating agencies are considering ways to protect the earth from asteroids.

The U.S. space agency, NASA, is also working with private partners to encourage the commercial use of space. Possible areas of revenue include using robots to mine asteroids, launching and maintaining communications satellites, and biomedical research. Space tourism may be another new space-based industry if Elon Musk's company SpaceX succeeds. In a private-public partnership with NASA, the company has already launched a rocket that delivered cargo to the International Space Station and safely returned to Earth. In the future, people may go for vacations on the moon as routinely as they now go to the seashore.

English Language Arts

Summarize Using Central Ideas and Key Details
Reading: Informational Text

Strategy   Use features in the passage, such as subheadings, to identify important ideas.

Test Tip   What do the two subheadings tell you about the way human exploration of space has changed?

1. **Based on the subheadings, what is the main way human exploration of space has changed?**

   (A) The United States is now leading the space race.

   (B) Astronauts are no longer the only people who can travel into space.

   (C) Different countries are now racing to reach Mars instead of the moon.

   (D) Nations are now working with other nations and private companies to explore space.

2. **The author explains the future of space exploration by**

   (A) giving examples of current and planned projects.

   (B) listing important events in the order they occurred.

   (C) making predictions about the future of space travel.

   (D) quoting astronauts who participated in historic events.

3. **How is space exploration today different than it was in the early days of the space race? Use at least two examples from the passage to support your answer.**

   _____

   _____

   _____

   _____

   _____

   _____

   _____

   _____

   _____

   _____

   _____

   _____

   _____

   _____

   _____

   _____

English Language Arts

Analyze Interactions Between Individuals, Events, and Ideas
Reading: Informational Text

DIRECTIONS: Read the passage. Then, answer the questions on the next page.

The Invention Factory at Menlo Park

Thomas Edison may be best known for inventing the first light bulb that could be mass-produced. But the incandescent bulb was only one of his 1,093 patents. His other inventions included a voting machine, a record player, and a movie projector.

One reason for Edison's success was his work ethic. His early attempts to find a material that would conduct electricity in a light bulb failed. A visitor to his lab said it was a shame that after all his work, he had gotten no results. Edison supposedly replied, "Results! Why, man, I have gotten a lot of results! I know several thousand things that won't work."

Edison was also good at inventing useful things people wanted to buy, like batteries and a telegraph system that could send two messages at once. In 1877, he proposed that Western Union pay for a laboratory where he could work with his assistants and be free of interruptions. In return, he would give the company a share of the profits on inventions developed there. He set a goal of producing "a minor invention every ten days and a big thing every six months or so."

His plan was so successful that Edison became famous as "the Wizard of Menlo Park." With the help of his assistants, he was able to work on many ideas at once. At times, up to 60 people worked in teams that researched and built everything from microphones to underground cables. Although his staff was hard-working and capable, they depended on Edison for new ideas. If he became ill, his assistants didn't have enough to do.

Edison never got a patent on his "invention factory" but his plan is still producing new ideas. Menlo Park inspired the research and development laboratories where companies invent and develop new products today.

English Language Arts

Analyze Interactions Between Individuals, Events, and Ideas

Reading: Informational Text

Strategy To find interactions, identify cause-and-effect relationships in the passage as you read.

Test Tip As you read, look for ways Edison influenced other inventors.

1. **How did Edison's work ethic contribute to his success?**

   (A) He was not easily discouraged.

   (B) He had a talent for sales.

   (C) He obtained patents on his ideas.

   (D) He was able to hire good people.

   Write how you know.

   _____

   _____

   _____

   _____

   _____

   _____

2. **How did Edison encourage the development of new ideas? Choose the three best answers.**

   (A) He focused on just a few ideas at a time.

   (B) He worked with others to develop his ideas into new products.

   (C) He refused to waste time on ideas that took too long to develop.

   (D) He created a model for research and development that is still used today.

   (E) He set an example of learning from every experiment, whether it worked or not.

   (F) He held a record number of patents, which inspired others to try to break his record.

3. **How is Edison still inspiring inventors today? Give at least two reasons for your answer. Base your reasons on details from the passage.**

   _____

   _____

   _____

   _____

   _____

   _____

   _____

   _____

   _____

   _____

   _____

Analyze Text Structure
Reading: Informational Text

DIRECTIONS: Read the passage. Then, answer the questions on the next page.

Yellowstone's Natural Wonders

The oldest national park in the United States, Yellowstone covers an area of land approximately 60 by 50 miles. Most of the park is located in the state of Wyoming, but it also spreads into Idaho and Montana. Yellowstone is the site of some of the most famous natural wonders in the world. Each year, more than 3 million visitors come to see its geysers, hot springs, and other natural wonders.

Scientists believe that the landscape of Yellowstone was created by a series of volcanic eruptions thousands of years ago. Molten rock, called *magma*, remains under the park. The heat from the magma produces the 200 geysers and thousands of hot springs for which Yellowstone is known.

Geysers

Geysers may differ in frequency of eruption and size, but they all work in much the same way. As water seeps into the ground, it collects around the hot magma. The heated water produces steam, which rises through cracks in the ground and pushes up the cooler water above it. When the pressure becomes too great, the water erupts into the air. The cooled water falls back to the ground, and the cycle begins again. Of all the geysers in Yellowstone, the most famous is Old Faithful. Approximately every 65 minutes, Old Faithful erupts for three to five minutes. The geyser sends a burst of boiling water 100 feet into the air.

Hot Springs

The magma under the park also produces bubbling hot springs and mud pools, called *mudpots*. Unlike geysers, hot springs do not erupt because the water is not under pressure. When hot water reaches the surface, it cools and sinks. More hot water then rises to the surface, which keeps the circulation going. The largest hot spring in Yellowstone, Grand Prismatic Spring, measures 370 feet wide.

Other Attractions

Evergreen forests of pine, fir, and spruce trees cover 90 percent of Yellowstone Park. Two hundred species of birds are found in Yellowstone. More than 40 kinds of other animals live in Yellowstone, which is the largest wildlife preserve in the United States. Visitors to the park may see bears, bison, cougars, moose, and mule deer. In addition, the park offers more than 1,000 miles of hiking trails.

Analyze Text Structure
Reading: Informational Text

Strategy | While reading, identify sentences that give a preview of what the article will cover. Authors of informational passages often introduce the topics they will cover in the first paragraph.

Test Tip | Often, the last sentence of the first paragraph previews the passage. What topics will be covered in this passage?

1. **According to the introduction, the three things the author plans to cover in this article are geysers, hot springs, and** _____

_____.

2. **Geysers are covered first in the passage because**
   - (A) the most popular attraction at Yellowstone is Old Faithful.
   - (B) they are the first topic mentioned in the preview sentence.
   - (C) scientists know more about geysers than they do the other attractions.
   - (D) the author finds them more interesting than the other natural wonders.

   Write how you know.

   _____

   _____

   _____

3. **Why is the second paragraph included?**
   - (A) to give details about how geysers work
   - (B) to show why Old Faithful is so popular
   - (C) to emphasize the difference between geysers and hot springs
   - (D) to explain why Yellowstone has so many geysers and hot springs

Write how you know.

_____

_____

_____

_____

_____

_____

4. **Which feature could be added to this passage?**
   - (A) How to get to Yellowstone National Park.
   - (B) Attractions to avoid when visiting.
   - (C) A list of all of the geysers and hot springs.
   - (D) Ways to keep safe when viewing wildlife.

   Write how you know.

   _____

   _____

   _____

   _____

5. **The third and fourth paragraphs each begin by explaining how something works. In what way are the endings of these paragraphs alike?**

   _____

   _____

   _____

Determine Author's Point of View or Purpose
Reading: Informational Text

DIRECTIONS: Read the passage. Then, answer the questions on the next page.

The Best of Both Breeds

What's not to love about a Labradoodle? American Labradoodles are cross-breeds between the Labrador retriever and the poodle. As a result, they have characteristics of both breeds. If you want an intelligent, friendly dog with a thick, wavy, non-allergenic coat, why not have a breeder create a Labradoodle puppy just for you?

A breeder would probably tell you there is no reason not to order a designer dog. If you love pugs, but don't want your dog to have trouble breathing, you might cross a pug with a beagle. The puppy will likely have a pug's cute face and fun-loving personality with a beagle's slightly longer nose.

According to breeders, cross-breeding can correct genetic problems that affect certain breeds. For example, German shepherds and other larger breeds can suffer from hip dysplasia. This condition causes painful or crippling wear on the hip joint. In addition, cross-breeds are said to be healthier than pure-bred dogs—their mix of genes gives them hybrid vigor.

Nevertheless, some think that the best way to get hybrid vigor is to find a rescue dog at an animal shelter. For one thing, there's no guarantee that cross-breeding will produce exactly the dog you want. For example, crossing a Yorkshire Terrier with a Teacup Poodle may produce a tiny Yorkipoo that will weigh about 5-9 pounds. On the other hand, terriers vary in size, which means their offspring may inherit their height.

Puppies can inherit the best traits of both parents. However, they may also inherit their worst traits. In that case, instead of correcting genetic defects, cross-breeding may produce a puppy that suffers from one or more health conditions. A puggle may inherit intelligence, but it may also be just as stubborn as its pug and beagle parents.

When you consider that prices for designer dogs begin at $700, the best place to find a great canine companion with hybrid vigor isn't at a breeder's, but at your local animal shelter.

English Language Arts

Determine Author's Point of View or Purpose
Reading: Informational Text

> **Strategy**   Read carefully to identify language that shows which side of an issue a writer is on. A writer's word choice can provide clues to his or her purpose.

> **Test Tip**   Phrases like *On the other hand* and *Nevertheless* signal when an author moves from one side of the argument to another side.

1. **Which statements from the passage express the author's opinion about designer dogs? Choose the three best answers.**

   (A) "If you want an intelligent, friendly dog with a thick, wavy, non-allergenic coat, why not have a breeder create a Labradoodle just for you?"

   (B) ". . . cross-breeding can correct genetic problems that affect certain breeds."

   (C) ". . . there's no guarantee that cross-breeding will produce exactly the dog you want."

   (D) "Puppies can inherit the best traits of both parents."

   (E) "However, they may also inherit their worst traits."

   (F) ". . . the best place to find a great canine companion with hybrid vigor isn't at a breeder's, but at your local animal shelter."

> **Test Tip**   Sometimes an author will include arguments on more than one side of a question. When this happens, look for ways the author proves the other side is wrong.

3. **The author includes arguments for and against designer dogs. In your opinion, does that make the author's opinion more or less credible? Give reasons for your answer.**

   _____

   _____

   _____

   _____

   _____

   _____

   _____

   _____

2. **Complete the chart by filling in the blanks.**

Argument for Designer Dogs	Why Author Thinks This Argument Is Wrong	Do You Agree or Disagree with Author?
Hybrids are healthier.		
You can get the dog you want.		
Cross-breeding can correct genetic defects.		

Name _____ Date _____

English Language Arts

Evaluate Arguments and Claims
Reading: Informational Text

DIRECTIONS: Read the informational article. Then, answer the questions on the next page.

The Benefits of Physical Activity

Regular physical activity is one of the most important things you can do for your health. It can help reduce your risk of some diseases, improve your mental health and mood, and increase your chances of living longer.

Protect Your Health

Getting at least 150 minutes (2 hours and 30 minutes) a week of moderate-intensity aerobic activity can put you at a lower risk for many serious diseases. You can reduce your risk even further with more physical activity.

Heart disease and stroke are two of the leading causes of death in the United States. Regular physical activity can cut your risk of developing heart disease by 45%. The protective effect against stroke isn't as easy to quantify. However, several studies show that inactive people are at higher risk for stroke. Exercise also helps stroke victims recover.

Being physically active lowers your risk for two types of cancer: colon and breast. Research shows that physically active people have a lower risk of colon cancer than sedentary people. Physically active women have a lower risk of breast cancer than people who are not active. Although the research is not yet final, some findings suggest that those who get regular physical activity lower their risk of endometrial cancer and lung cancer.

Improve Your Mental Health and Mood

Regular physical activity can help keep your thinking skills sharp as you age. It can also reduce your risk of depression and may help you sleep better. Research has shown that doing aerobic or a mix of aerobic and muscle-strengthening activities 3 to 5 times a week for 30 to 60 minutes can give you these mental health benefits. (Aerobic exercises like running, swimming, or cycling stimulate your heart and lungs.) Some scientific evidence has also shown that even lower levels of physical activity can be beneficial.

Live Longer

Few lifestyle choices affect your health as much as physical activity. People who are physically active for about 7 hours a week have a 40 percent lower risk of dying early than those who are active for less than 30 minutes a week. You don't even have to exercise for hours or at a high level of intensity to reduce your risk of premature death. You can put yourself at lower risk of dying early by doing at least 150 minutes a week of moderate-intensity aerobic activity.

Evaluate Arguments and Claims
Reading: Informational Text

Strategy   While reading, decide whether a claim is valid by judging the strength and relevance of the evidence that supports it.

Test Tip   To help you judge a claim, look for evidence to support each claim an author makes.

1. **Part A: Which statement accurately summarizes the author's claim about how exercise affects your chances of dying early?**

   (A) Any type of exercise reduces your risk of early death by 40%.

   (B) Even moderate exercise for 2.5 hours a week reduces your risk of early death.

   (C) Intense exercise for 7 hours a week might cut your risk of premature death in half.

   (D) Light exercise for about 3 hours a week can cut your risk of premature death by nearly 50%.

   Part B: What type of evidence is used to support this claim?

   (A) personal experience

   (B) individual success stories

   (C) scientific research of active and inactive people

   (D) DNA analysis of people who have lived a long time

Part C: Why is a story about how one person who exercised regularly and lived an amazingly long time not enough to support this claim?

_____

_____

_____

_____

_____

_____

2. **The author summarizes the results of several studies about the effect of exercise on stroke risk because**

   (A) the scientists who did the studies collected no statistics.

   (B) the statistical results were too complicated for researchers to analyze.

   (C) the results of the studies varied too much for researchers to narrow them down to just one statistic.

   (D) the scientists who did the studies were looking for qualitative data on lifestyle instead of quantitative statistics.

English Language Arts

Evaluate Arguments and Claims
Reading: Informational Text

Strategy — Decide whether a claim is valid by evaluating whether the evidence that supports it comes from credible sources.

Test Tip — Evidence that comes from an expert source is generally more credible than evidence from someone without expert knowledge or professional credentials.

3. Suppose that after finishing the article on "The Benefits of Physical Activity," the author found a claim about an additional benefit of exercise: Students who are physically active get better grades. If this claim were added to the article, which would be the best evidence to support it?

(A) Your cousin Anton is more active than his brother Darren, and Anton gets higher grades.

(B) Several studies have found that students who are fit and active in middle school are more likely to be fit, happy adults.

(C) The American College of Sports Medicine reports in a 2006 study that students who were active for at least 20 minutes three days a week got better grades than students who did less exercise.

(D) The author of a popular blog advises all her readers to get at least 30 minutes of exercise each day, even if the exercise has to be broken into smaller chunks throughout the day.

4. Explain the criteria you used to decide which piece of evidence in question 3 was the most credible. In other words, give the reason that made you choose your answer. Also give reasons for not choosing the other answer choices.

_____

_____

_____

_____

_____

_____

_____

5. If you wanted to find additional evidence to back up this claim, which source is likely to provide the most credible evidence?

(A) an article on "Health" in Wikipedia

(B) a study published by two exercise researchers at a university

(C) a DVD by an actress who has developed her own fitness program

(D) a TV news story about how reducing recess time has affected grades in your school system

English Language Arts

Evaluate Arguments and Claims
Reading: Informational Text

DIRECTIONS: Read the passage. Then, answer the questions that follow.

Can Exercise Cure Insomnia?

If you decide to hit the gym in hopes that a quick dose of exercise will cure your insomnia, a new study suggests that will not be enough. While adopting an exercise program *did* ultimately help some insomniacs sleep better, the scientists found it didn't happen right away.

"My patients were coming in and saying that they heard that exercise is good for sleep," explained study author Kelly Baron, director of the Behavioral Sleep Medicine Program at Northwestern University in Chicago. "But people generally want a quick fix. And they weren't seeing improvements right way. So, they were getting discouraged."

"The message here is that exercise is not a quick fix, which I don't really think is discouraging at all," Baron said. "Our previous work found that exercise over a 16-week period is very effective in promoting sleep. . . . But like with weight loss or any sort of behavioral change, it doesn't happen immediately. You have to measure progress over months, not day-to-day."

Baron and her colleagues published their latest findings online in the *Journal of Clinical Sleep Medicine*.

Strategy Identify the claim or point an author makes. Then, find at least two details that support that claim, or make it valid.

6. The author of a blog entry used the results of Dr. Baron's study to support the claim that exercise will cure insomnia. Write the sentence from the passage that proves this claim is exaggerated.

_____

_____

_____

_____

_____

_____

7. Give at least two reasons that Dr. Baron can be considered a credible source.

_____

_____

_____

_____

_____

_____

_____

_____

_____

English Language Arts

Analyze How Two Authors Present Information

Reading: Informational Text

DIRECTIONS: Read the article. Then, answer the questions that follow.

Strategy | Read each passage separately to understand its main ideas and purpose. Then, reread to focus on similarities and differences in the way the authors treat the same topic.

Paul Revere's Ride

"Listen my children and you shall hear. Of the midnight ride of Paul Revere," begins the famous poem by Henry Wadsworth Longfellow. Longfellow recounts the events of April 18, 1775, when silversmith Paul Revere galloped from Boston to Concord to warn the rebels that British troops were marching to seize their weapons.

This wasn't Revere's first ride for the Liberty Boys, a group that gathered information about British attempts to stop the colonies from rebelling. In 1774, he rode to Oyster River, NH, to warn that the British planned to seize the fort there. Members of the local militia retrieved and hid gunpowder from the fort. That gunpowder was later used in the Battle of Bunker Hill.

His warning to the Minutemen of Lexington and Concord was also successful. The weapons stored in these towns were moved before the British could capture them.

Revere ended his midnight ride by securing a trunk full of papers that could be used to accuse Patriot leaders of treason before the evidence fell into British hands. According to the CIA, most people think of Revere as just "a guy on a horse." However, he is "arguably the most famous military intelligence agent from the American Revolution."

1. **According to the article, why was Paul Revere important to the colonists' fight for liberty?**

   (A) Longfellow, a well-respected poet, wrote a famous poem about him.

   (B) Revere was captured by the enemy, but managed to escape from his captors.

   (C) Revere's warning kept the weapons hidden at Lexington and Concord from being captured by the British.

   (D) Revere carried out several missions that kept the Patriots' weapons and their leaders safe from British soldiers.

Analyze How Two Authors Present Information
Reading: Informational Text

Strategy — While reading, identify the author's purpose in order to analyze the information presented.

Test Tip — An author's purpose is to entertain, to inform, or to persuade. If an author is giving information, ask yourself why the author wants you to know this information. If the author is trying to persuade you to agree with his or her idea, ask yourself if the details are convincing enough.

2. The tone of this article could best be described as _____.

(A) admiring

(B) critical

(C) neutral

(D) reverent

Write how you know.

_____

_____

_____

_____

_____

3. How does the author attempt to show that Revere is more than "just 'a guy on a horse' "?

_____

_____

_____

_____

_____

_____

_____

_____

_____

4. Based on this article, would you say that Revere deserves to be recognized as an American hero? Give at least two reasons for your answer.

_____

_____

_____

_____

_____

_____

_____

Analyze How Two Authors Present Information

Reading: Informational Text

DIRECTIONS: Read the article. Then, answer the questions that follow.

Strategy Compare the two accounts and identify how the authors write about the same subject yet emphasize different evidence.

Sybil Ludington: The Female Paul Revere

Paul Revere gets most of the credit for riding to warn the Patriots that the British were coming to seize the weapons they had stored in Lexington and Concord. But Revere was not the only rider that night. William Dawes and Dr. Samuel Prescott also rode to warn the villages around Boston that the Redcoats were marching. All three were captured by British patrols, but all managed to escape.

Another Patriotic rider is almost unknown to history. Yet she rode 40 miles through wooded backcountry roads (compared to Revere's 14-mile ride) without getting captured. Her name is Sybil Ludington, and she was the sixteen-year-old daughter of the militia commander in Kent, Connecticut.

On April 26, 1777, a rider brought word that the British had attacked Danbury and local militia troops were needed to defend the nearby town. Because it was planting season, Colonel Ludington's troops were all on their farms working to get crops in the ground. The rider was exhausted and not sure he could find the widely scattered farms in the dark. Fortunately, Sybil knew the countryside. She rode through the night, carrying the news from Kent to Mahopac to Stormville. The militia gathered at daybreak to begin the march to Danbury. Although they couldn't stop the British from burning warehouses and destroying supplies desperately needed by Washington's troops, the 400 Patriots did force 2,000 British Redcoats to retreat to Long Island Sound.

5. **Compare this author's presentation of information about Paul Revere's ride to the first author's presentation. Identify at least two differences.**

_____

_____

_____

_____

_____

_____

_____

6. **The author suggests that Sybil Ludington deserves at least as much recognition as Paul Revere. Cite two pieces of evidence from the article to support this inference.**

_____

_____

_____

_____

_____

_____

_____

English Language Arts

Understand Word Relationships
Language

DIRECTIONS: Read each short passage. Then, answer the question that follows.

Strategy — Analyze a variety of strategies to understand how words are related in a passage. Look at details, context, and word clues.

What looks like a liquid but shatters like glass? The answer: a non-Newtonian fluid, which can be either a liquid or a solid. For example, a mix of cornstarch and water can be used to fill potholes. The mixture acts like a liquid until pressure is applied to it. Then, the mixture becomes solid enough that cars can drive over it.

1. **Which figure of speech is used to describe non-Newtonian fluids?**
   - (A) hyperbole
   - (B) metaphor
   - (C) personification
   - (D) simile

Using quotations in a paper you are writing is much like the process of making a sandwich. When you make a sandwich, you first lay a piece of bread flat to provide a foundation for the filling. Then, you add ingredients like peanut butter and jelly. Finally, you put another piece of bread on top to hold everything together. When you use a quotation in your writing, you lay the foundation by first stating the point you want to prove. Then, you add the quotation to the middle of the paragraph. Finally, you write something about the quotation that helps the reader understand how it helps support your point. The words you quote become the "filling" in your quotation sandwich.

2. **What figure of speech is used to describe the process of using someone else's words in your paper?**
   - (A) analogy
   - (B) hyperbole
   - (C) metaphor
   - (D) personification

NASA's Dragon spacecraft, launched with the Falcon 9 rocket, has nine engines in the first stage and one in the second stage. The Dragon carries supplies to the International Space Station.

3. **Which definition of the word *stage* is most likely correct in this context?**
   - (A) area in a theater
   - (B) step in a process
   - (C) detachable unit
   - (D) profession of performing in plays

Test Tip

Look for word choices that signal bias in the sources you use. If a source gives inaccurate information, it may be an honest mistake. It may also be a sign that the source is biased.

Understand Word Relationships
Language

Strategy Read the sentences and identify the main idea or topic. Then, find the meaning of the unknown word that makes sense with the main idea or topic.

Paul Revere's engraving of the Boston Massacre is not entirely accurate. For example, he gave the Royal Custom House a new name: Butcher's Hall. His drawing of the conflict between the colonists and armed British troops is thus an example of persuasion.

4. Which of the words below has almost the same meaning as *persuasion*, but with a more negative connotation?

Ⓐ encouragement

Ⓑ evidence

Ⓒ myth

Ⓓ propaganda

Strategy

Use what you know about root words to figure out the meaning of unfamiliar words.

Test Tip

Search the Internet for a list of root words and their meanings and use the list to study for your test.

The root word *counter* means "opposite" or "contrary."

5. When you include a *counterargument* in your writing, what do you do?

_____

_____

_____

_____

_____

"When I study something," said Jerusha, "I like to break it down into parts so I can take time to understand each part."

6. What is another word for the study strategy Jerusha uses?

Ⓐ analyze

Ⓑ compare

Ⓒ contrast

Ⓓ debate

Write an Argument
Writing

Strategy   When you are asked to write an argument, state your position and back it up with evidence.

Test Tip   An argument is more convincing if you support your opinion with facts and reasons.

DIRECTIONS: Choose a topic that reasonable people might disagree on. You might propose a change to a school policy or take a stand on what we need to do about climate change. Then, complete the organizer by writing your answers for each step in the space provided.

STEP 1: Make a claim.

My claim:

STEP 2: Consider the evidence.

My list of evidence for my claim:	My list of evidence against my claim:

STEP 3: Organize your evidence logically. For example, you might use time order or order of importance. Begin each item on your list with transition words, such as *first* or *most important*.

1.

2.

3.

STEP 4: Write a conclusion that sums up what you want your reader to do or to remember.

My conclusion:

English Language Arts

Write an Argument
Writing

DIRECTIONS: Read the passage. Then, answer the questions that follow.

> [1] Although some skeptics deny that climate change is happening, its effects are already being felt on several Pacific Islands. [2] If sea levels continue to rise at their current rate, several low-lying countries could be underwater by 2100. [3] Coastal farmland on the outer islands of Fiji has already been ruined by salt water. [4] The government is building desalination plants and making plans to move people inland. [5] The people of Kiribati expect they may need to pack up their bags and head on out of town. [6] They have already purchased land where all 100,000 of them could find a new home.

1. **The first sentence is an example of how to**

   (A) use statistics as evidence.

   (B) state your claim in one sentence.

   (C) preview each main point of your argument.

   (D) acknowledge arguments that can be made against your claim.

2. **Rewrite sentence 5 so it matches the formal tone of the rest of the passage.**

   _____

   _____

   _____

   _____

   _____

3. **Write a conclusion to an argument paper on climate change. If you support the idea of climate change, you may write a conclusion for the passage. If you disagree with the passage, write a conclusion that expresses your point of view on climate change.**

   _____

   _____

   _____

   _____

   _____

   _____

   _____

   _____

   _____

   _____

Write an Informative Text
Writing

Strategy Plan the structure of your informative passage before you begin to write. Common structures are main idea and details, cause and effect, and problem-solution.

DIRECTIONS: A student wrote an informative essay about the Great Barrier Reef. Read the paragraph from the informative essay. Then, answer the questions.

> Can you imagine a wilderness under the sea that is so humongous it has never been fully explored? The Great Barrier Reef is such a place because it is the largest ridge of coral in the world. It is 1,250 miles long—that's about as far as the distance between Detroit, Michigan, and Houston, Texas. Its undersea coral gardens provide homes for more than 1,400 varieties of exotic fish. This huge maritime province stretches along the northeastern coast of Australia and ranges from 10 to more than 100 miles from the shore.

1. **What structure did the student use to organize this introductory paragraph?**

   (A) compare-contrast

   (B) space order

   (C) time order

   (D) order of importance

2. **Write the sentence in which the student used a transition word to signify a cause-effect relationship.**

   _____

   _____

   _____

   _____

3. **Most of the language the student uses is formal. How would you rewrite the first sentence to replace the informal expression with more formal language?**

   _____

   _____

   _____

4. **Why did the student compare the length of the Great Barrier Reef to the distance between two cities?**

   _____

   _____

   _____

5. **If the student wanted more information on the Great Barrier Reef, which three search terms would return the most information? Choose the best three answers.**

   (A) cays

   (B) coral reefs

   (C) Great Barrier Reef

   (D) Great Barrier Reef Marine Park

   (E) large green turtles

   (F) World Heritage Site listing for Great Barrier Reef

English Language Arts

Write an Informative Text
Writing

Strategy | Take notes to support your main ideas with relevant details. When taking notes, you must put words taken directly from the source in quotation marks. Try to use your own words—paraphrase—as much as you can.

6. Part A: A search for "Great Barrier Reef facts" returned lists of facts from several sources. Which source would be the most credible?

(A) Easy Science for Kids

(B) Great Barrier Reef Marine Park Authority

(C) Great Adventures—Cairns Tours

(D) HowStuffWorks.com

Part B: Explain your answer to Part A.

_____

_____

Test Tip
When paraphrasing this sentence, you do not need to quote the names of the endangered species that live there.

The UNESCO World Heritage Site has this description of the Great Barrier Reef: "It also holds great scientific interest as the habitat of species such as the dugong ('sea cow') and the large green turtle, which are threatened with extinction."

7. The student paraphrased this quotation this way: According to UNESCO, this coral ecosystem provides a home for several endangered species, including the sea cow and the large green turtle. Explain why this is a good paraphrase of this material.

_____

_____

Test Tip
If you have trouble paraphrasing a source, start with an idea from the middle or at the end. Remember that any words you take directly from the source must be put in quotation marks, except for technical terms.

Within the GBR there are some 2,500 individual reefs of varying sizes and shapes, and over 900 islands, ranging from small sandy cays and larger vegetated cays, to large rugged continental islands rising, in one instance, over 1,100 meters above sea level. Collectively these landscapes and seascapes provide some of the most spectacular maritime scenery in the world.

8. How might this quotation be paraphrased?

_____

_____

_____

_____

_____

_____

_____

_____

_____

English Language Arts

Write an Informative Text
Writing

DIRECTIONS: Write three paragraphs about the Great Barrier Reef or another topic. Include the following:

- Information from at least two sources
- Facts about your topic
- Definitions and examples to help readers understand your topic
- A correctly formatted list of all the sources you used at the end

Plan your informative article by looking up at least two sources on your topic. Then, choose an organizational plan (cause-effect, compare-contrast, time order, etc.). Use your organizational plan to put your notes in order.

_____

_____

_____

_____

_____

_____

_____

_____

_____

_____

_____

_____

_____

_____

_____

_____

_____

_____

_____

_____

_____

_____

Name _____ Date _____

English Language Arts

Write a Narrative
Writing

DIRECTIONS: Read the fable. Then, answer the questions.

[1] The North Wind and the Sun argued as to which was the most powerful, and agreed that whoever could get the cloak off a Traveler would be the winner. [2] The North Wind first tried his power and blew with all his might, but the more he blew, the closer the Traveler wrapped his cloak around him. [3] Resigning all hope of victory, the Wind called upon the Sun to see what he could do. [4] The Sun suddenly shone out. [5] The Traveler no sooner felt his genial rays than he took off first his hat, and then, his cloak.

Strategy

Plan a narrative writing by deciding on characters, setting, and plot events. Who will be in your story, and what conflict will they face? How will they resolve the conflict?

1. **What does the first sentence do?**

   (A) foreshadow the ending

   (B) describe the time and the place

   (C) establish a first-person point of view

   (D) introduce the characters and the conflict

2. **Which phrase could be added to sentence 3 to create a better connection with sentence 2?**

   (A) At last,

   (B) Even if,

   (C) Instead,

   (D) On the other hand,

Test Tip

You can use narrative techniques, such as dialogue and descriptive details, to make stories more interesting.

3. **Rewrite sentence 4 so that it includes descriptive details.**

   _____

   _____

   _____

   _____

4. **Sentence 3 summarizes a conversation between the Wind and the Sun. Replace sentence 3 with dialogue between these two characters.**

   _____

   _____

   _____

   _____

   _____

   _____

5. **Fables usually end with a moral that states the lesson readers are intended to learn. Write a moral for this fable.**

   Moral: _____

   _____

   _____

Write a Narrative
Writing

DIRECTIONS: Read the paragraph. A narrative is a story that tells about real or imagined events. Write a narrative about a new product that greatly improves your life. The product can be real or imagined. Write your paragraph on the lines. Your paragraph should have the following:

- A narrator and/or characters
- A natural sequence of events
- Dialogue
- Descriptions of actions, thoughts, and feelings
- Time words and phrases to show the order of events
- Concrete words and sensory details
- A sentence to end your paragraph

Strategy Plan a narrative by choosing people, places, and events that will be in the story. Use an outline to keep your ideas organized and to make sure you have details.

Test Tip Choosing the right words makes a narrative more interesting to read. Use exact words and phrases and figurative language.

_____

_____

_____

_____

_____

_____

_____

_____

_____

_____

_____

_____

_____

_____

_____

_____

Strategy Review

DIRECTIONS: Each strategy below is followed by a review, a passage, and one or more questions. Use these to review important strategies.

Strategy Use details from the story or poem to make inferences, understand theme, and draw out meaning.

A theme can be a lesson learned. For example, a fable ends with a moral that is directly stated. However, a theme can also be a general view of life, as in the story of "The Three Little Pigs."

One pig builds his house of straw, another of sticks, and a third of bricks. Two of the pigs build their houses the quick and easy way; only the one who plans for the future survives.

Reread these lines from "The Little Black-Eyed Rebel."

**"With the news of loved ones absent to
the dear friends they would greet,
Searching them who hungered for them,
swift she glided through the street.
'There is nothing worth the doing
that it does not pay to try,'
Thought the little black-eyed rebel,
with a twinkle in her eye."**

1. **Reread the passage from "The Little Black-Eyed Rebel." Then, state a theme of the poem in your own words.**

   _____

   _____

   _____

   _____

   _____

Strategy

As you read, identify literary or structural elements and use them to understand the meaning of a story or poem.

A *genre* is a type of literature, such as poetry or drama. Recognizing genres helps you understand how to interpret a story, poem, or passage.

Read the poem "The Cloud," by Percy Bysshe Shelley.

**I am the daughter of Earth and Water,
    And the nursling of the Sky;
I pass through the pores of the ocean and shores;
    I change, but I cannot die.**

2. **Choose three things that tell you that "The Cloud" is a poem.**
   (A) Rhyming words follow a pattern.
   (B) The ocean doesn't really have pores.
   (C) The lines follow a pattern of rhythm.
   (D) It is written from the cloud's point of view.
   (E) The language is figurative rather than literal.
   (F) Words like "Earth" and "Water" are capitalized.

Strategy Review

Strategy Reread passages to make comparisons, draw conclusions, or support inferences.

VISITOR: *"Mr. Edison, what a shame that after all your work, you've gotten no results."*

EDISON: *"Results! Why, man, I have gotten a lot of results! I know several thousand things that won't work."*

This quotation is famous because it illustrates one reason for Edison's success: he was not easily discouraged. How do we know? He chose to learn from failure instead of giving up. The author does not explain this directly, but leaves it to readers to draw this conclusion about Edison. Reread this part of the passage:

Edison was also good at inventing useful things people wanted to buy, like batteries. . . . In 1877, he proposed that Western Union pay for a laboratory. . . . In return, he would give the company a share of the profits on inventions developed there.

3. **Part A: What can readers infer about Edison, based on this excerpt?**

   (A) He was very productive.

   (B) He was not an honest person.

   (C) He was a good businessman.

   (D) He inspired others to be creative.

   Part B: Cite a detail from the excerpt that supports your answer to Part A.

   _____

   _____

   _____

   _____

Strategy

Use word clues in a passage to identify its structure, to see how ideas in a passage are related, and to clarify word meanings.

When it's time for a monarch caterpillar to turn into a butterfly, the first step is to find a safe place to make a cocoon. The caterpillar secretes silk to make a pad on the underside of a branch. Then, it hooks itself to the branch and sheds its skin to reveal a chrysalis. Inside this protective casing, the pupa reshapes itself into the adult butterfly that will eventually emerge.

Transitions are words or phrases that show how ideas are connected. Words like *before*, *following*, or *next* can signal how events are related in time. Transitions like *because* or *as a result* can show a cause-effect relationship. Use an Internet search for "transition words" to find lists of many more transitions.

4. **Write a phrase from the model that identifies the beginning of the transformation process.**

   _____

Context clues are words or phrases within a passage that help you understand unfamiliar words. Sometimes the writer will make the definition obvious by using phrases like *The word* phantasmagorical *means "dreamlike" or "imaginary."* In other cases, you must find hints to the word's meaning in the sentences close to it.

5. **Write the phrase from the model that helps you find the meaning of the word *chrysalis*.**

   _____

Strategy Review

Strategy When writing, use details to support, explain, or clarify your main ideas.

The PBS website ZOOMsci challenges readers to make a Rube Goldberg™ machine. The challenge: Design a machine that puts toothpaste on a toothbrush in at least twenty steps. Why twenty steps? That's because cartoonist Rube Goldberg is famous for his drawings of machines that performed simple tasks in complicated ways.

Details can be either helpful or distracting. If your readers have never seen a Rube Goldberg machine, adding relevant details can help them understand these wacky inventions. However, adding details that don't relate to the main idea may confuse readers.

6. **Choose three details that could be added to the model paragraph to help readers understand how a Rube Goldberg machine works.**

(A) Rube Goldberg's full name was Reuben Garrett Lucius Goldberg.

(B) Rube Goldberg was a professional cartoonist for 60 years.

(C) One of his Weekly Inventions has a series of gears, a bucket, a crab, an exhaust pipe, and a small bellows that all work together to blow sand out.

(D) Rube Goldberg studied engineering and his first job was working as a mining engineer.

(E) Goldberg's machines often involve live animals.

(F) You can see examples of Rube Goldberg machines in the Gallery at RubeGoldberg.com.

Strategy

Use an outline to plan your writing.

Scratch Outline for an Argument

STEP 1: Make a claim.

My claim: *Wind energy is a green energy source that could replace fossil fuels.*

STEP 2: Consider the evidence.

My list of evidence for my claim:	My list of evidence against my claim:
1. *Wind power does not cause pollution.*	1.
2. *Wind turbines could produce more than 20 times the electricity needed by the entire planet.*	2. *We do not have cost-effective ways to store wind energy*
3. *Wind power is growing at 25% per year since 2010.*	3.

Conclusion: *The U.S. should develop ways to produce wind energy on a larger scale.*

While you can do a formal outline, complete with Roman numerals *I*, *II*, and *III*, often a scratch outline is enough. These outlines get their name from the way they're written—very quickly and informally, maybe even scratched on the back of an outline. A quick look at Robbie's outline above shows that his arguments are not balanced.

7. **Based on the outline, what does Robbie need to do before drafting his argument on wind energy?**

_____

_____

_____

_____

Strategy Review

Strategy Use transitions to show how ideas are related in an argument.

People usually assume that cats purr because they're happy. In reality, the sound is far more complex. Cats purr when recovering from injury, and scientists suspect the sound helps strengthen their bones. Cats also purr when they want food. In fact, some have perfected a "manipulative meow," which embeds a sound like a baby's cry inside their normal low-frequency purr. They use the sound to influence humans to give them food.

When your assignment is to write an argument, you may be asked to include a *counterargument*. A counterargument is an argument against your position. One reason to include a counterargument is to give you a chance to show why the other side is wrong. To do this, you need to use transitions that signal disagreement. Transitions that show contrast include *but*, *on the other hand*, *actually*, or *the truth is*.

8. Write the phrase from the model that is used to contrast the counterargument and what the author believes to be the truth.

_____

Strategy Revise to make sure your writing is clear and makes sense. Then, edit to fix errors.

Students often assume that good writers get their drafts right the first time. Actually, most professional writers agree with Roald Dahl that "good writing is essentially rewriting." How do you know what to rewrite? Reading your writing aloud will help you find awkward places that need smoothing. Neil Gaiman advises setting your work aside, then reading it "as if you've never read it before. If there are things you aren't satisfied with as a reader, go in and fix them as a writer: that's revision."

9. Write another revision tip that could be added to the model.

_____

_____

_____

_____

10. Which of the following sentences contains incorrect punctuation?

Ⓐ Tina never worried, about the weather.

Ⓑ The fast-moving rabbit escaped the hungry fox.

Ⓒ The following animals are mammals: dogs, cats, and hamsters.

Ⓓ Grandfather rakes the leaves; later, he dumped them into the compost pile.

Strategies for Mathematics Tests

Read the strategies below to learn more about how they work.

Use rules, properties, or formulas to solve problems.

You can use rules, properties, and formulas to solve a variety of problems. For example, if you know the formula for the area of a rectangle, you can use a given length and width of the rectangle (or a rectangular garden) to quickly find its area. If you understand the commutative and distributive properties, you can rearrange an equation to solve it. If you understand the rules of the order of operations, you can correctly evaluate a mathematical expression.

Use drawings, graphs, or number lines to understand and solve a problem.

Many problems on a test can be modeled with a quick sketch, graph, or number line. These drawings can help you visualize the problem, figure out what you are being asked to find, or solve word problems.

Read word problems carefully to identify the given information and what you are being asked to find.

Whenever you encounter a word problem, you should first ask *What is the given information?* Then, you should ask *What question am I being asked to answer?* or *What am I being asked to find?* Don't start your calculations until you know the answers to these questions!

Look for key words in word problems that help you know which operation to use.

Key words in problems are signals that you should use certain operations. For example, the words *how much less* indicate subtraction. The words *total* and *altogether* often indicate addition. If you are asked to split something into equal portions, use division.

Organize and display data in order to interpret it.

Interpreting data means finding meaning in it. One way to find meaning in data is to organize it in a visual way. For example, dot plots are great for understanding data from a survey or poll. Line graphs show how two sets of data are related.

Apply prior knowledge and basic operations to solve problems.

As you work through the pages in this workbook, you will see strategies like the ones on this page. Using what you already know about numbers and about the basic operations addition, subtraction, multiplication, and division, you can solve problems involving decimals, fractions, geometry, and converting units of measurement. For example, you can use your understanding of division, multiplication, and place value to find area and to convert meters to centimeters.

Write and solve equations to solve real-world problems.

Translating everyday language into equations that use numbers, variables, and operations signs is an essential strategy. You will need to combine your understanding of several strategies to write and solve these equations, including understanding basic operations; applying rules, properties, and formulas; and looking for clues in the words to find needed information.

Compute Unit Rates
Ratios and Proportional Relationships

DIRECTIONS: Solve each problem.

Strategy Find unit rates by dividing rational numbers.

Test Tip Read directions and each question carefully so you know how to answer.

1. Makaela runs $\frac{1}{4}$ mile in 3 minutes. If she continues at the same speed, how long will it take her to run one mile?

_____

Draw and label a picture showing why your answer makes sense.

2. Pedro can mow $\frac{2}{3}$ of an acre of his lawn in $\frac{1}{2}$ an hour. How many acres can Pedro mow in an hour?

_____

Draw and label a picture showing why your answer makes sense.

3. Jack hikes $\frac{3}{10}$ of a mile of a trail in $\frac{1}{3}$ of an hour. What is the unit rate?

Ⓐ $\frac{1}{10}$ mile per hour

Ⓑ $\frac{9}{10}$ mile per hour

Ⓒ $1\frac{1}{9}$ miles per hour

Ⓓ $\frac{1}{10}$ hour per mile

4. A painter completes $\frac{2}{3}$ of a job in $\frac{3}{4}$ of a day. What is the unit rate?

Ⓐ $\frac{8}{9}$ of the job per day

Ⓑ $\frac{1}{2}$ of the job per day

Ⓒ $\frac{5}{7}$ of the job per day

Ⓓ $1\frac{1}{8}$ of the job per day

5. In problem 4, which answer choice can you eliminate without doing any calculations? Write how you know.

_____

_____

6. Elliott works at a bakery. He can frost and decorate $\frac{1}{2}$ of a cake in $\frac{1}{3}$ of an hour. How many cakes can Elliott decorate in an hour? Show your work.

Identify Proportional Relationships
Ratios and Proportional Relationships

DIRECTIONS: Use the tables below to solve each problem.

Strategy   Use ratios to determine if two quantities are in a proportional relationship. The ratios will be equal to each other.

Test Tip   Remember to answer all parts of the question.

1. **Rupal types 55 words per minute. Complete the table.**

Time (in minutes)	1	2	3	4
Number of Words	55			

Complete the ratios.

$$\frac{\text{Words}}{\text{Time}} = \frac{55}{1} = \_\_\_\_ = \_\_\_\_ = \_\_\_\_ = \_\_\_\_$$

Is the relationship between the number of words and the time a proportional relationship? Write how you know.

_____

_____

_____

_____

2. **The table shows the time it took a biker to ride certain distances. Tell whether the relationship is a proportional relationship. Write how you know.**

Time (in hours)	1	2	3	4
Biking Distance (in miles)	12	24	33	44

_____

_____

_____

_____

3. **The table below shows the cost of renting DVDs. Tell whether the relationship is a proportional relationship. Write how you know.**

Number of DVDs	2	3	5	7
Cost	6	9	15	21

_____

_____

_____

_____

_____

_____

Identify Unit Rates
Ratios and Proportional Relationships

DIRECTIONS: Use the graph to answer questions 1 and 2.

Strategy   Use a graph or a table to find the unit rate. On a graph, the unit rate is at (1, *r*).

Test Tip   Read directions and each question carefully so you know how to answer.

Trail Mix

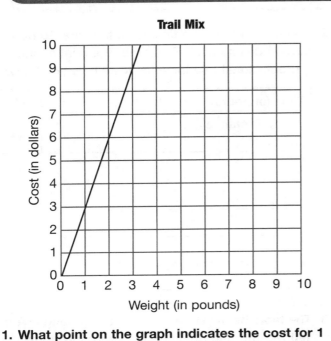

Weight (in pounds)

1. **What point on the graph indicates the cost for 1 pound of trail mix?**

_____

2. **Use the graph to find how much it costs for 1 pound of trail mix. Write how you know.**

_____

_____

_____

DIRECTIONS: Use the table to answer questions 3 and 4.

Jamie's Wages

Time (in hours)	2	3	4	5
Wages	$16	$24	$32	$40

3. **What is the unit rate for Jamie's wages? Write how you know.**

_____

_____

_____

_____

_____

_____

4. **If you continued the table and graphed its data, which of the following points would not be on the graph?**

   (A) (9, 72)

   (B) (11, 88)

   (C) (13, 104)

   (D) (17, 156)

Represent Proportional Relationships
Ratios and Proportional Relationships

DIRECTIONS: Choose or write the correct answer.

Strategy Use the equation for a proportional relationship between x and y written as $y = ax$, where a is a positive number.

Test Tip In some multiple choice questions, you can check your answer by substituting each value into the equations.

1. On a road trip, Keisha drives 120 miles in 2 hours, 150 miles in 3 hours, and 210 miles in 3.5 hours. Complete the table.

Time (in hours)	2	3	3.5
Distance Driven (in miles)	120		

Complete the ratios to find the common ratio.

$\dfrac{\text{Distance}}{\text{Time}} = \dfrac{120}{2} = $ _____ = _____ = _____

Let x represent the time in hours. Let y represent the distance driven in miles. Use the common ratio as the constant of proportionality. The equation for the relationship is _____ .

2. Ryder reads 8 pages in 32 minutes, 12 pages in 48 minutes, 15 pages in 60 minutes, and 25 pages in 100 minutes. Write an equation for the relationship. Tell what the variables represent.

_____

_____

_____

3. Joshua earns $26 for mowing 2 lawns, $65 for mowing 5 lawns, and $91 for mowing 7 lawns. Which equation represents this relationship if x is the number of lawns mowed and y is the amount earned?

(A) $y = 26x$
(B) $y = 91x$
(C) $y = -13x$
(D) $y = 13x$

4. Nori drove 64 miles on 2 gallons of gas, 160 miles on 5 gallons of gas, and 256 miles on 8 gallons of gas. Which equation represents this relationship if x is the number of gallons of gas used and y is the miles driven?

(A) $y = 64x$
(B) $y = 32x$
(C) $y = 256x$
(D) $x = 256y$

5. Sylvia is selling raffle tickets. The table shows the prices of different numbers of tickets.

Tickets	5	10	25
Cost Driven	$10		

Use the data in the table to find the common ratio. Then, write an equation that represents the proportional relationship. Identify all variables used.

_____

_____

Use Proportions
Ratios and Proportional Relationships

DIRECTIONS: Choose or write the correct answer.

Strategy | Use proportions to solve multistep ratio and percent problems.

Test Tip | After you finish the problem, reread the problem and check that you answered the question correctly.

1. Marco works in a home improvement store for $8.00 per hour. If his pay is increased to $10.00, then what is the percent increase in his pay?

   The amount of increase in Marco's pay is _____ .

   To find the percent increase, divide the amount of increase by the original pay.

   $$\frac{10-8}{8} = \frac{\boxed{}}{8} = \frac{\boxed{}}{\boxed{}} = \underline{} \%$$

2. An electronics store buys a camera from a supplier for $80 and marks up the price by 50%. The salesman gets a commission of 15% of the selling price of the camera. How much commission will the salesman receive? Write how you know.

   _____

   _____

   _____

   _____

3. A softball team won $\frac{3}{4}$ of the 56 games it played one season. How many games did the team lose?

   (A) 14
   (B) 25
   (C) 31
   (D) 42

4. Josie bought a new jacket that cost $65. The sales tax was 6%. How much did Josie pay for the jacket including sales tax?

   (A) $3.90
   (B) $61.10
   (C) $65.06
   (D) $68.90

5. Braden bought a computer on sale for 18% off its original price. The original price was $695. What was the price of the computer after the discount? Show your work.

Name _____ Date _____

Math

Absolute Value and Opposite Integers
The Number System

DIRECTIONS: Choose or write the correct answer.

1. Use the number line to answer the questions.

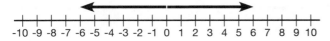

-10 -9 -8 -7 -6 -5 -4 -3 -2 -1 0 1 2 3 4 5 6 7 8 9 10

How far is 6 from 0 and in which direction?

_____

What is the opposite of 6?

_____

How far is −6 from 0 and in which direction?

_____

The sum of 6 and its opposite, −6, is _____ .

2. Write an integer to describe each situation. Then, give the situation and integer that describes the opposite situation. Finally, write the absolute value of the integer.

3 degrees below zero

Integer: _____

Situation, Opposite Integer:

_____

Absolute Value: _____

a gain of 8 yards in a football game

Integer: _____

Situation, Opposite Integer:

_____

Absolute Value: _____

3. Explain why a deposit of $20 and a withdrawal of $20 are opposite quantities.

_____

_____

4. |7| + |−8| = ☐

   Ⓐ −1

   Ⓑ −15

   Ⓒ 1

   Ⓓ 15

5. |25| = ☐

   Ⓐ −25

   Ⓑ 25

   Ⓒ 5

   Ⓓ 50

6. Solve and show your work.

|−9| + |−7| − |5| × |−2|= ☐

Add and Subtract Integers
The Number System

DIRECTIONS: Choose or write the correct answer.

Strategy   Use number lines or rules to add and subtract integers.

Test Tip   Write down the rules for adding and subtracting integers before you start.

1. Garrett owes his friend Taylor $4. If he borrows another $3, how much will he owe Taylor altogether?

Owing $4 can be represented by _____ .

Owing $3 can be represented by _____ .

The problem can be solved by adding −4 + −3. Draw a number line from −10 to 10 and use it to find the sum.

Start at 0. Move _____ to the left. Then, move 3 to the _____ .

Since −4 + − 3 = _____ , Garrett will owe Taylor _____ .

2. The temperature at noon was 8°F. By 6:00 P.M., the temperature had dropped 10°. What was the temperature at 6:00 P.M.?

Since 8 + (−10) = _____ , the temperature at 6:00 P.M. will be _____ .

3. −6 + −2 = _____

4. 13 + (−9) = _____

5. 12 − (−3) = ☐
   - (A) −15
   - (B) −9
   - (C) 9
   - (D) 15

6. −7 + 7 = ☐
   - (A) −14
   - (B) 0
   - (C) 14
   - (D) 49

7. Tobiah starts with $125.00 in her bank account. On Saturday, she withdraws $35.00 to buy books for school. On Monday, she deposits $20.00 in babysitting money. On Tuesday, the bank charges her a $3 monthly fee. How much money is in her account at the end of Tuesday? Show your work.

Add and Subtract Rational Numbers

The Number System

DIRECTIONS: Choose or write the correct answer.

Strategy   Extend rules for adding and subtracting integers to all rational numbers.

Test Tip   Remember that you can rewrite a subtraction expression as an addition expression: $4.6 - (-0.8) = 4.6 + (0.8)$.

1. Find $2\frac{3}{4} + 1\frac{2}{3}$.

_____

Explain how you found your answer.

_____

_____

_____

_____

_____

_____

_____

_____

2. Find $4.58 + (-6.25) - (-1.67)$. Show your work.

3. $-\frac{2}{3} + 4\frac{1}{6} = \boxed{}$

   (A) $3\frac{1}{2}$

   (B) $4\frac{5}{6}$

   (C) $-3\frac{1}{2}$

   (D) $-4\frac{5}{6}$

4. $6.07 - (-3.94) = \boxed{}$

   (A) -2.13

   (B) 2.13

   (C) -10.01

   (D) 10.01

Use Properties
The Number System

DIRECTIONS: Choose or write the correct answer.

Strategy | Apply properties of operations as strategies to perform operations with rational numbers.

Test Tip | The **commutative property** says you can switch the order of the numbers and still get the same answer. The **associative property** says you can change the grouping of the numbers and still get the same answer. The **distributive property** is used when there is a combination of multiplication over addition or subtraction.

1. Simplify $-4\frac{5}{6} + 3.2 - \frac{1}{6}$.

$-4\frac{5}{6} + 3.2 - \frac{1}{6}$

$= -4\frac{5}{6} + 3.2 + (-\frac{1}{6})$ since subtracting a number is the same as adding its _____.

$= -4\frac{5}{6} + (-\frac{1}{6}) + 3.2$ by the _____ Property of Addition.

$= (-4\frac{5}{6} + (-\frac{1}{6})) + 3.2$ by the _____ Property of Addition.

$=$ _____ $+ 3.2$

$=$ _____

DIRECTIONS: For questions 2–3, use the properties of operations to evaluate each expression.

2. $7.8 - 2\frac{7}{8} - (-3.2)$

_____

What property did you use to evaluate the expression?

_____

3. $6(4\frac{2}{3} - 2\frac{1}{2})$

_____

What property did you use to evaluate the expression?

_____

4. Shar uses the Associative Property to help her evaluate the expression $9 - (8 + \frac{1}{3}) + \frac{2}{3}$. Which expression did she evaluate?

Ⓐ $9 + (8 + \frac{1}{3} + \frac{2}{3})$

Ⓑ $9(8) + (\frac{1}{3} + \frac{2}{3})$

Ⓒ $(9 - 8) + (\frac{1}{3} + \frac{2}{3})$

Ⓓ $\frac{2}{3} + 9 + \frac{1}{3} - 8$

Multiply and Divide Integers
The Number System

DIRECTIONS: Complete the charts by using a pattern.

Strategy   Use a pattern or rules to multiply and divide integers.

1.

4 × 3 =	12
4 × 2 =	8
4 × 1 =	4
4 × 0 =	
4 × −1 =	
4 × −2 =	
4 × −3 =	

−4 × 3 =	
−4 × 2 =	
−4 × 1 =	
−4 × 0 =	
−4 × −1 =	
−4 × −2 =	
−4 × −3 =	

12 ÷ 4 =	3
8 ÷ 4 =	2
4 ÷ 4 =	1
0 ÷ 4 =	
−4 ÷ 4 =	
−8 ÷ 4 =	
−12 ÷ 4 =	

−12 ÷ 4 =	
−8 ÷ 4 =	
−4 ÷ 4 =	
0 ÷ 4 =	
4 ÷ 4 =	
8 ÷ 4 =	
12 ÷ 4 =	

3. The product of two positive integers or two negative integers is a _____ integer.

Example: _____

_____

4. The quotient of a positive integer and a negative integer is a _____ rational number.

Example: _____

_____

5. The quotient of two positive integers or two negative integers is a _____ rational number.

Example: _____

_____

DIRECTIONS: Complete each statement. Then, give an example.

Test Tip

Remember that multiplying and dividing are opposite operations.

2. The product of a positive integer and a negative integer is a _____ integer.

Example: _____

_____

6. −9 × 3 × (−4) = ☐

Ⓐ −10
Ⓑ 10
Ⓒ −108
Ⓓ 108

7. −72 ÷ (−3) ÷ −4 = ☐

Ⓐ −6
Ⓑ 6
Ⓒ −65
Ⓓ 65

Use Rational Numbers in the Real World
The Number System

DIRECTIONS: Read the information below. Then, answer the questions.

Strategy   Use the properties of rational numbers to help you solve problems.

Test Tip   Remember to include the units in your final answer.

1. A recipe calls for $1\frac{3}{4}$ cups of sugar. Stacy only has a $\frac{1}{4}$ cup measuring cup. How many times will she need to fill the measuring cup?

   What operation is called for? _____

   Write an expression to solve the problem.

   _____

   Change the mixed number to an improper fraction and divide.

   $$1\frac{3}{4} \div \frac{1}{4} = \frac{\boxed{}}{4} \div \frac{1}{4} = \frac{1}{4} \times \frac{\boxed{}}{\boxed{}} = \underline{}$$

   Stacy will need to fill the measuring cup _____ times.

2. The drama club has a budget of $600 for their annual play. The club can spend no more than $\frac{3}{8}$ of the money on new costumes. How much money is budgeted for costumes? Show your work.

   _____

3. Marley uses $4\frac{2}{5}$ yards of cloth to make a costume for the play. How many yards of cloth will Marley need to make 3 costumes?

   Ⓐ $12\frac{1}{5}$ yards

   Ⓑ $12\frac{4}{5}$ yards

   Ⓒ $13\frac{1}{5}$ yards

   Ⓓ $13\frac{4}{5}$ yards

4. Justin bought 21 yards of material to make drapes. He paid $6.95 per yard. How much did Justin spend on material for the drapes? Show your work.

   _____

   _____

5. A bag contains 30 cups of dog food. Joshua's dog eats $1\frac{1}{2}$ cups of dog food each day. How many days will the bag of dog food last?

   Ⓐ 15 days

   Ⓑ 20 days

   Ⓒ 30 days

   Ⓓ 35 days

Multiply and Divide Rational Numbers
The Number System

DIRECTIONS: Choose or write the correct answer.

Strategy   Use properties of operations as strategies to multiply and divide rational numbers.

1. Find the product: $4 \times 3\frac{5}{8}$

$4 \times 3\frac{5}{8} = 4 \times (3 + \underline{\hspace{1.5cm}})$

$= (4 \times 3) + (4 \times \underline{\hspace{1.5cm}})$ by the **Distributive Property**

$= \underline{\hspace{1.5cm}} + \underline{\hspace{1.5cm}}$

$= \underline{\hspace{1.5cm}}$

DIRECTIONS: Fill in the blank with = or ≠. Explain your choice.

2. $-1\frac{2}{3} \times 6 \underline{\hspace{1.5cm}} 6 \times -1\frac{2}{3}$

_____

_____

_____

3. $-\frac{15}{5} \underline{\hspace{1.5cm}} -\frac{5}{15}$

_____

_____

_____

4. $-25 \times 6.3 \times 4 \underline{\hspace{1.5cm}} (-25 \times 4) \times 6.3$

_____

_____

_____

DIRECTIONS: Use properties of operations to find each product or quotient. Then, identify the property used.

5. $\frac{3}{5}(-29) + \frac{3}{5}(-16)$

_____

6. $\frac{5}{8} \div (-\frac{5}{8})$

_____

7. -2.5×10.4

_____

Convert Rational Numbers to Decimals

The Number System

DIRECTIONS: Solve each problem.

Strategy   Use division to convert a fraction to a decimal.

Test Tip   Use a grid when solving long division problems so that you line up the numbers correctly.

EXAMPLE: Write $\frac{3}{8}$ as a decimal.

Divide 3 by 8.

Add a 0 after the decimal point.

Subtract 24 from 30.

Add zeroes in the dividend and continue dividing until the remainder is 0.

The decimal for $\frac{3}{8}$ is 0.375. This is a terminating decimal.

$$
\begin{array}{r}
.375 \\
8\overline{)3.000} \\
-24 \\
\hline
60 \\
-56 \\
\hline
40 \\
-40 \\
\hline
0
\end{array}
$$

1. Write $\frac{5}{11}$ as a decimal. Tell if it is a terminating or repeating decimal.

3. Jenna uses division to convert $\frac{7}{8}$ to a decimal. She says that it converts to a repeating decimal. Is she correct? Why or why not? Show your work.

2. Write $\frac{9}{16}$ as a decimal. Tell if it is a terminating or repeating decimal.

_____

_____

Solve Real-World Problems
The Number System

DIRECTIONS: Solve each problem.

Strategy | Apply properties of operations to calculate with numbers in any form.

Test Tip | Read word problems carefully for the numbers you will use in your calculations.

1. **Paul earns $15 per hour. He receives a 10% raise. Write an expression that shows how he can calculate his new hourly pay rate.**

   10% written as a fraction is _____ .

   Paul's new hourly pay rate will be

   $15 + _____ ($15)

   Calculate his new hourly pay rate.

   $15 + _____ ($15) = $15 + _____ = _____

2. **Mindy goes out to eat with a friend. The cost of their meal is $25.62 which includes a tax of $1.22. Mindy only wants to leave a 20% tip based on the cost of the food.**

   Write an expression that shows how she can calculate the amount of the tip.

   _____

   Find the amount of the tip, rounded to the nearest dollar. Write how you know.

   _____

   _____

   _____

3. **The table below shows Yui's scores for the first 5 holes of a golf game. What is Yui's average score for the 5 holes?**

Hole	1	2	3	4	5
Score	−2	−1	−3	0	1

   Ⓐ 1
   Ⓑ $1\frac{1}{4}$
   Ⓒ −1
   Ⓓ −5

   Test Tip

   When problems involve real-world situations and details, think about whether your answer is reasonable.

4. **Rochelle borrows $6,900 from her parents to buy a car. She pays her parents $250 each month until the loan is paid off. Write an expression to calculate how long it takes Rochelle to pay her parents back. Then, solve the expression. Show your work.**

Math

Evaluate Expressions
Expressions and Equations

DIRECTIONS: Evaluate the following expressions if $w = \frac{1}{2}$, $y = 5$, and $z = -3$. Show your work.

Strategy Use the order of operations and properties to evaluate expressions using given values.

Test Tip Remember PEMDAS when using order of operations: Parentheses, Exponents, Multiplication and Division, Addition and Subtraction.

EXAMPLE
$$y(6w + 4z) = 5(6 \times \tfrac{1}{2} + 4 \times -3)$$
$$= 5(3 + -12)$$
$$= 5(-9)$$
$$= -45$$

1. $3y + 4z - 2w =$ _____

2. $4(w - 2z) + 6 \div 2 =$ _____

3. $z(2w + y) =$ _____

4. What is the value of $2(a + b) - 9c$ if $a = 7$, $b = -2$, and $c = \frac{1}{3}$?
   - (A) 4
   - (B) 7
   - (C) 9
   - (D) 15

5. What is the value of $(p + q)6r + 2q + p$ if $p = 4$, $q = -5$, and $r = \frac{1}{3}$?
   - (A) −4
   - (B) −8
   - (C) −16
   - (D) 12

6. Which operation symbol makes the following equation true?

   $6(2 + 8)$ ☐ $10 \div 5 = 58$
   - (A) −
   - (B) +
   - (C) ÷
   - (D) ×

7. Which operation symbol makes the following equation true?

   $7(8 - 3)$ ☐ $210 \div 6 = 0$

Simplify Expressions
Expressions and Equations

DIRECTIONS: Fill in the blanks to solve the problem.

Strategy Apply properties of operations as strategies to simplify linear expressions.

1. Find the sum of $3x + 7$ and $2x$.

   An expression that shows the sum of $3x + 7$ and $2x$ is _____ .

   $(3x + 7) + 2x = 3x + (7 + 2x)$ by the _____ **Property of Addition.**

   $3x + (7 + 2x) = 3x + (2x + 7)$ by the _____ **Property of Addition.**

   $3x + (2x + 7) = (3x + 2x) + 7$ by the _____ **Property of Addition.**

   $(3x + 2x) + 7 =$ _____ **because** $3x$ and $2x$ are _____ **terms and can be combined.**

DIRECTIONS: Choose or write the correct answer.

2. Simplify the expression $-3m + 2 - 5m - 3$.

   _____

3. Simplify the expression $6(b - 7)$.

   _____

4. Simplify the expression $5(2x) - 4y(8)$.

   _____

5. Which expression is equivalent to $10(x - 2)$?
   - (A) $7x - 8 + 3x + 12$
   - (B) $7(x + 8) + 3(x + 12)$
   - (C) $7(x - 8) + 3(x - 12)$
   - (D) $7(x - 8) + 3(x + 12)$

6. Which expression is equivalent to $-16p + 28q$?
   - (A) $-4(4p - 7q)$
   - (B) $8(2p) - 4(-7q)$
   - (C) $-8(-2p) - 4(-7q)$
   - (D) $-4(4p + 7q)$

7. Simplify the expression $9(a + 3) + 9(b - 4)$. Show your work.

Rewrite Expressions
Expressions and Equations

DIRECTIONS: Read the information below. Then, complete the statements.

Strategy   Rewrite an expression in different forms to show how the quantities in it are related.

Test Tip   Look for key words to help you solve a word problem. If someone gets a raise in wages, the new rate will be greater than the old one. If something is on sale, its new price will be less than the old price.

1. Sydney is getting a 3% raise to her hourly pay. Write an expression that represents her new hourly pay rate.

   Sydney's hourly pay rate will increase by _____%, which is _____ written in decimal form.

   If Sydney's current hourly pay is h, then her new hourly pay will be $h +$ _____ .

   $h + 0.03h = 1h + 0.03h =$ _____

DIRECTIONS: Choose or write the correct answer.

2. A bike store is having a 20% off sale. Write an expression that represents the cost of buying a bike that is on sale at the store.

   _____

3. A camera store marks up the cost of a camera by 35%. Which expression represents the price that the camera sells for?
   - (A) 0.35c
   - (B) 1.35c
   - (C) 35c
   - (D) $\frac{c}{35}$

4. Tell if the statement is true or false.

   An increase by 15% is the same as multiplying by 1.15. _____

   A 25% discount is the same as finding 75% of the cost. _____

   A markup by 40% is the same as multiplying by 1.04. _____

5. A department store offers 25% off any small appliance. Suzanne has a coupon for $5 off any purchase. If a coffee maker normally sells for $45, write an expression that represents how much will it cost Suzanne after both the sale discount and the coupon.

   _____

   _____

Solve Problems with Linear Equations
Expressions and Equations

Strategy   Solve multistep equations by identifying the operations involved and undoing them in the opposite order.

Test Tip   Substitute your answer into the original problem to check.

DIRECTIONS: Use the problem below to complete the statements with the correct operations and solve the equation.

1. Carl bought some CDs for $8 each and a DVD for $11. He spent a total of $83. How many CDs did Carl buy? Use c to represent the number of CDs that Carl bought.

The equation that represents the situation is

_____

Operations in equation	To solve	Solving the equation
First, c is _____ by 8.	First, _____ 11 from both sides of the equation.	$8c + 11 = 83$ $8c + 11$ _____ $= 83$ _____ $8c = $ _____
Then, 11 is _____.	Then, _____ both sides by 8.	$\dfrac{8c}{\boxed{}} = \dfrac{72}{\boxed{}}$ $c = $ _____

DIRECTIONS: Choose or write the correct answer.

2. The Beach Hut rents umbrellas for $19 plus $4 per hour. Leah paid $39 to rent an umbrella. For how many hours did she rent the umbrella? Write an equation.

_____

Use the equation to solve.

_____

3. A baker made 5 batches of muffins. He sells 6 muffins to a customer and has 34 muffins left. How many muffins were in each batch? Which equation could be used to solve?

- (A) $5 - 6b = 34$
- (B) $5 + 6b = 34$
- (C) $5b - 6 = 34$
- (D) $5b + 6 = 34$

Solve Problems with Linear Equations

Expressions and Equations

Strategy   Read multistep equations carefully to identify the operations involved.

Test Tip   Look for key words that relate to operations, such as *total*, *spent*, *used*, *earned*, *increased*, and *multiplied*.

DIRECTIONS: Solve the problem below by writing the equation and using the correct operations to solve the equation.

4. Mara grew so many tomatoes that she decided to sell some at the farmer's market. She will sell each small box of tomatoes for $4 and one large box of tomatoes for $8. She earned a total of $64. How many small boxes did Mara sell? Use *b* to represent the number of small boxes that Mara sold.

   The equation that represents the situation is

   _____

   Write the order of operations to solve the equation.

   _____

   _____

   Solve the equation. Show your work and explain each operation.

DIRECTIONS: Write the correct answer.

5. Joanie has $38 when she arrives at the amusement park. After she buys 6 ride tickets, she has $20 left. What is the price of each ride ticket? Write and solve an equation.

   _____

   _____

6. Max spends half of his allowance bowling. He washes the family car and earns $5. What is his weekly allowance if he ends up with $12? Write and solve an equation.

   _____

   _____

Solve Linear Inequalities and Graph the Solution Set

Expressions and Equations

> **Strategy**   Write, solve, and graph an inequality and interpret the solution within the context of the problem.

> **Test Tip**   Remember to reverse the inequality sign when multiplying or dividing both sides of an inequality by a negative number.

1. Eloise needs $23 to buy a new calculator. Her mother agrees to pay her $5 an hour for cleaning up the basement in addition to her $8 weekly allowance. What is the minimum number of hours Eloise must work to have enough money to purchase the calculator?

Write an inequality to represent the situation.

_____

_____

Solve the inequality. _____

So, Eloise must work at least _____ hours.

Graph the solution to the inequality.

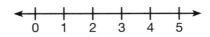

2. Tim will have his birthday party at the bowling alley with some friends, but the most he can spend is $75. The bowling alley charges a flat fee of $25 for a private party and $8 per person for shoe rentals and unlimited bowling. The birthday person bowls for free. What is the greatest number of friends Tim can invite? Write and solve an inequality. Then, graph the solution.

_____

_____

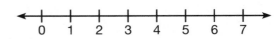

3. Caleb has $6. Rolls cost $0.80 each and a container of margarine costs $1.50. If Caleb buys one container of margarine, how many rolls can he buy? Write how you know.

_____

_____

_____

_____

_____

_____

Solve Linear Inequalities and
Graph the Solution Set
Expressions and Equations

Strategy To solve an inequality, find all values of the variable that make the inequality true.

4. Which number line shows the solution to the inequality $-2x - 3 > -1$?

(A)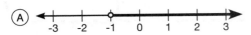

(B)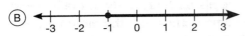

(C)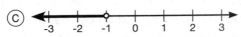

(D)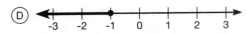

5. On this number line, shade all the points on the line where $x \geq 5$.

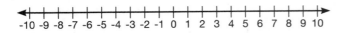

6. On this number line, shade all the points on the line where $x \leq 6$.

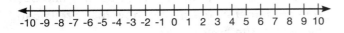

7. On this number line, shade all the points on the line where $x + 3 < -3$.

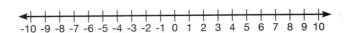

8. On this number line, shade all the points on the line where $-4 < x < 9$.

9. On this number line, shade all the points on the line where $x + 1 < -4$.

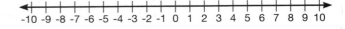

Use Plane Sections
Geometry

DIRECTIONS: Choose or write the correct answer.

> ## Strategy
> Use the characteristics of two- and three-dimensional figures to identify plane figures that are cross sections of three-dimensional figures.

1. **Two right triangular pyramids with cross sections are shown below. Complete the sentences.**

   The shape of the base is a _____,
   so the cross section of a plane parallel to the
   base is a _____.

   The shape of each side is a _____,
   so the cross section of a plane perpendicular to
   the base is a _____.

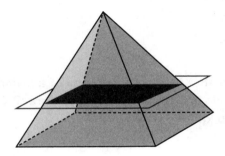

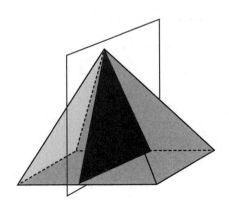

2. **Jan says that she can make a square, an equilateral triangle, and an octagon by using different cross sections of a cube. Is she correct? Explain.**

   _____

   _____

   _____

   _____

   _____

   _____

   _____

   _____

   _____

   _____

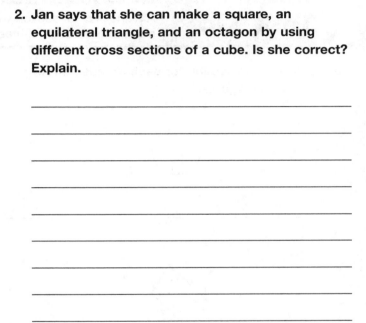

Use Plane Sections
Geometry

DIRECTIONS: Choose or write the correct answer.

Strategy Use the attributes of shapes to identify a given plane within a shape.

Test Tip A plane is a flat section within a shape. A cross-section is a shape made when a plane cuts through a three-dimensional shape.

3. **Name a cross section for each of these three-dimensional figures.**

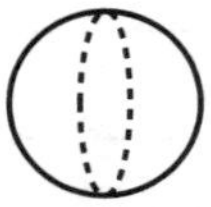

_____

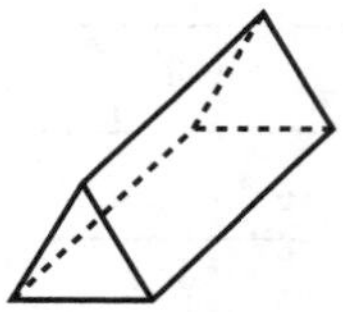

_____

_____

4. **Look at the figure below.**

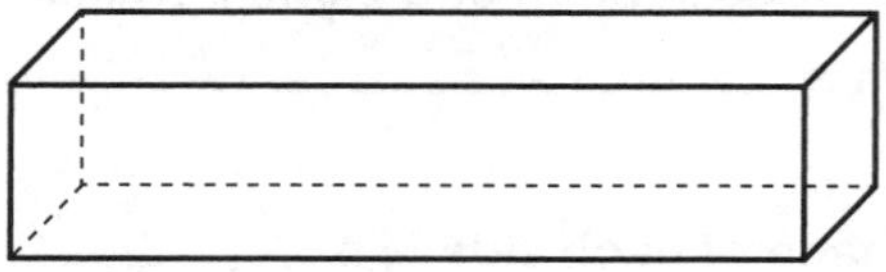

Which could not be a cross section?

(A) parallelogram

(B) rectangle

(C) square

(D) trapezoid

5. **Lily says that the cross sections of a cylinder can be a circle and rectangle. Do you agree? Write how you know.**

_____

_____

_____

_____

_____

Find Area of Circles
Geometry

DIRECTIONS: Choose or write the correct answer.

Strategy   Use the formula $A = \pi r^2$ to find the area of a circle.

Test Tip   Remember to include the correct units in the solution. The area of a figure is always in square units.

1. **A flower garden in the shape of a circle has a diameter of 6 feet. What is the area of the garden? Use 3.14 for π.**

   The formula for the area of a circle is $A = \pi r^2$.

   The diameter of the flower garden is 6 feet, so the radius is _____ .

   $A = \pi r^2 = 3.14 \times$ _____$^2 = 3.14 \times$ _____

   = _____ ft.²

2. **Find the area of each circle. Round to the nearest tenth, if necessary. Use 3.14 for π.**

   a circle with r = 10 in.

   _____

   a circle with r = 5 ft.

   _____

   a circle with d = 18 cm

   _____

3. **A CD has a radius of 6 cm. What is the area of the CD? Use 3.14 for π.**
   - (A) 6.28 cm²
   - (B) 59.18 cm²
   - (C) 113.04 cm²
   - (D) 452.16 cm²

4. **The base of a snare drum has an area of 153.86 in.² What is the diameter of the drum?**
   - (A) 7 in.
   - (B) 14 in.
   - (C) 24.5 in.
   - (D) 49 in.

Find Circumference of Circles
Geometry

DIRECTIONS: Choose or write the correct answer.

Strategy   Use the formulas $C = 2\pi r$ and $C = \pi d$ to find the circumference of a circle.

Test Tip   Remember to include the correct units in the solution. Units for circumference are often inches, feet, centimeters, or meters.

1. A round swimming pool has a diameter of 18 feet. What is the circumference of the pool? Use 3.14 for π.

   You are given the diameter, so use the formula for _____ to find the circumference.

   The diameter of the pool is 18 feet, so the radius is _____ .

   $C = \pi d = 3.14 \times$ _____ = _____ feet

2. Find the circumference of each circle to the nearest hundredth. Use 3.14 for π.

   circle with $r = 4$ m

   _____

   circle with $d = 7.5$ ft.

   _____

   circle with $r = 13$ in.

   _____

3. Abby has an exercise wheel with an 11 in. diameter for her guinea pig. What is the circumference of the exercise wheel to the nearest whole number? Use 3.14 for π.
   - (A) 17 in.
   - (B) 35 in.
   - (C) 69 in.
   - (D) 95 in.

4. Kai needs a new bicycle tire. His tire has a circumference of about 113.04 inches. What is the diameter of the tire?
   - (A) 6 in.
   - (B) 18 in.
   - (C) 36 in.
   - (D) 72 in.

Use Angle Relationships
Geometry

DIRECTIONS: Use the figure below to answer the questions.

Strategy | Use facts about supplementary, complementary, vertical, and adjacent angles in a multi-step problem to write and solve simple equations for an unknown angle in a figure.

Test Tip | Add to determine the type of angle. Two supplementary angles added together equal 180°. Two complementary angles added together equal 90°. Vertical angles are equal; if you know the measure of one, you can find the measure of the other.

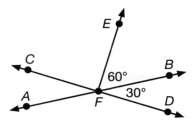

1. Name a pair of adjacent angles. Write how you know.

_____

_____

_____

_____

_____

2. Name a pair of vertical angles. Write how you know.

_____

_____

_____

_____

_____

3. Name a pair of complementary angles. Write how you know.

_____

_____

_____

_____

4. Name a pair of supplementary angles. Write how you know.

_____

_____

_____

_____

_____

5. What is the measure of ∠AFC? Write how you know.

_____

_____

_____

_____

_____

Use Angle Relationships
Geometry

DIRECTIONS: Use the figure to answer the questions.

Strategy — Read the word problems carefully to identify the measurements of angles you know and to make sure you know which angle measurement to solve for.

Test Tip — Remember that a full rotation of all angles forms a circle and equals 360°.

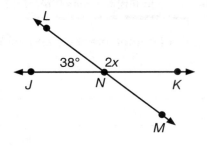

6. Find the measure of ∠KNM.

_____

Write how you know.

_____

_____

_____

_____

7. Find the measure of ∠JNM.

_____

Write how you know.

_____

_____

_____

_____

_____

_____

_____

8. Find the value of x. Show your work.

Use Angle Relationships
Geometry

DIRECTIONS: Use the figure below for problems 9 and 10.

DIRECTIONS: Use the figure below for problems 11 and 12.

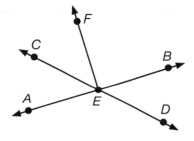

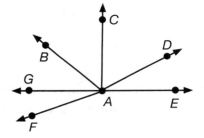

9. **Determine which of the following statements is false.**

   (A) ∠AEC and ∠BED are congruent.

   (B) ∠AED and ∠BEC are congruent.

   (C) ∠AEC and ∠AED are supplementary.

   (D) ∠AEF and ∠FEB are complementary.

   Write how you know.

   _____

   _____

   _____

   _____

∠CEF and ∠BED are congruent, and m∠FEB is twice m∠BED. What is the m∠FEB?

   (A) 30°

   (B) 45°

   (C) 90°

   (D) 120°

11. **∠CAE is a right angle. If the measure of ∠EAD is 28°, what is the measure of ∠CAD?**

   (A) 52°

   (B) 62°

   (C) 72°

   (D) 152°

   Write how you know.

   _____

   _____

   _____

12. **The measure of ∠BAE is 140° and the measure of ∠GAF is 20° less than the measure of ∠BAG. What is the measure of ∠GAF?**

   (A) 20°

   (B) 40°

   (C) 60°

   (D) 80°

Find Volume
Geometry

DIRECTIONS: Use the figures to complete the statements.

Strategy | Use the formula for the volume of a prism. The volume *V* of a prism is the area of its base *B* times its height *h*. So, *V* = *Bh*

Test Tip | Read all parts of the question first.

1.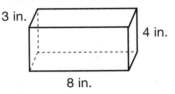

3 in.

4 in.

8 in.

The base is a _____ with a

length of _____ inches and a width of _____

inches.

The formula for the area of the base is *A* = *lw*, so

A = _____ in. × _____ in. = _____ in.²

V = *Bh* = _____ in.² × _____ in. = _____ in.³

2.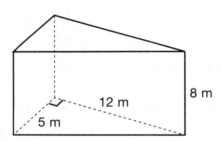

8 m

12 m

5 m

The base is a _____ with side

lengths of _____ meters and _____ meters.

The formula for the area of the base is $A = \frac{1}{2}bh$,

so $A = \frac{1}{2}$ _____ m × _____ m = _____ m²

V = *Bh* = _____ m² × _____ m. = _____ m³

3. A cube has a side length of 5 cm. What is the volume of the cube? Explain your answer.

(A) 10 cm³

(B) 15 cm³

(C) 25 cm³

(D) 125 cm³

_____

_____

_____

_____

_____

Find Volume
Geometry

Strategy | Use the formula for the volume of a cube. The volume *V* of a cube is the length *l* multiplied by its width *w* and height *h*. So, $V = l \times w \times h$

Test Tip | Remember that the volume of a solid figure is always expressed in cubic units.

4. What is the volume of the following right prism?

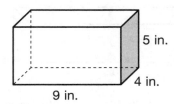

5 in.
4 in.
9 in.

- (A) 18 in.³
- (B) 41 in.³
- (C) 180 in.³
- (D) 90 in.³

5. What is the volume of a right prism with a length of 8 feet, a width of 2 feet, and a height of 6 feet?

- (A) 96 cubic feet
- (B) 18 cubic feet
- (C) 16 cubic feet
- (D) 32 cubic feet

6. What is the volume of the following triangular prism?

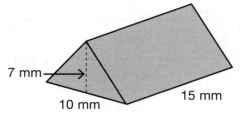

7 mm
10 mm
15 mm

- (A) 150 mm³
- (B) 525 mm³
- (C) 715 mm³°
- (D) 1,050 mm³

7. A model house is made by sticking a triangular prism on top of a rectangular block, as shown in the diagram. What is the volume of the model house?

- (A) 75 cm³
- (B) 150 cm³
- (C) 225 cm³
- (D) 300 cm³

4 cm
4 cm
12.5 cm
3 cm

Find Surface Area
Geometry

DIRECTIONS: Use the figures below to answer the questions.

> **Strategy** Use formulas for area and basic operations to find surface area. The surface area *SA* of a prism is the sum of the area of all its faces.

> **Test Tip** Remember that the surface area of a solid figure is always expressed in square units.

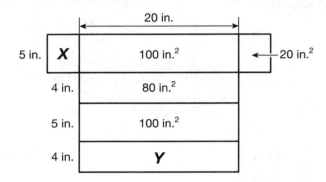

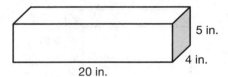

1. What is the area of side *X*?
- (A) 20 in.²
- (B) 40 in.²
- (C) 45 in.²
- (D) 100 in.²

2. What is the area of side *Y*?
- (A) 20 in.²
- (B) 40 in.²
- (C) 80 in.²
- (D) 100 in.²

3. Which of the following formulas shows how to find the surface area of the prism?
- (A) $SA = 100 + 80 + 20$
- (B) $SA = X + 100 + 80 + 20$
- (C) $SA = X + Y + 100 + 80 + 20$
- (D) $SA = X + Y + 100 + 100 + 80 + 20$

4. What is the surface area of the right prism?
- (A) 200 in.²
- (B) 400 in.²
- (C) 600 in.²
- (D) 800 in.²

Find Surface Area
Geometry

Strategy   To find surface area, use or draw the shape involved, carefully labeling the measurements you know from the word problem.

5. A box in the shape of a cube has a side length of 8 in. What is the surface area of the box? Write how you know.

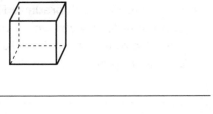

_____

_____

_____

6. You are wrapping a gift box that is 15 inches by 12 inches by 3 inches. What is the least amount of wrapping paper you need in order to wrap the box?

Ⓐ 30 in.²

Ⓑ 261 in.²

Ⓒ 522 in.²

Ⓓ 540 in.²

7. To find the surface area of a triangular prism, use the formula $SA = 2B + Ph$. B is the area of the base, P is the perimeter of the bases, and h is the height of the prism.

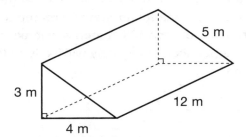

The area of the base, B, is _____ m².

The perimeter of the base, P, is _____ m.

The height of the prism, h, is _____ m.

Fill in the formula.

$SA = 2 \times$ _____ $+$ _____ $\times$ _____

The surface area of the triangular prism is

_____ .

8. The total surface area of the three rectangular faces of a right triangular prism is 92 cm². The total surface area of the prism is 134 cm². What is the area of each triangular base?

Ⓐ 21 cm²

Ⓑ 42 cm²

Ⓒ 47 cm²

Ⓓ 67 cm²

Understand Sampling
Statistics and Probability

DIRECTIONS: Explain your answers in complete sentences.

Strategy Gain information about a population by examining a sample of the population.

Test Tip Read each question carefully before deciding how to answer it.

1. In a random sample of 45 students in the school cafeteria, Alana found that 20 ordered a tuna wrap. If there are 405 students who eat the cafeteria lunch, how many will likely order a tuna wrap?

   _____

   _____

   _____

2. Is the sample in question 1 a good sampling of the population? Explain.

   _____

   _____

   _____

3. Why might you choose to use the sample survey rather than survey the entire population? Explain.

   _____

   _____

   _____

4. Evan took a survey of favorite types of books from a random sample of 30 students. The books are to be sold in a bookstore at a school with 750 students. Should the sample be larger? Explain.

   _____

   _____

   _____

5. A pre-election poll predicted that a certain candidate for mayor would receive 30% of the vote. He actually received 70%. Was this poll useful? Explain.

   _____

   _____

   _____

6. Give two reasons why the pre-election poll could have been so far off in question 5.

   _____

   _____

   _____

   _____

   _____

7. A poll is being taken at a middle school to determine whether to change the school colors. Which would be the best place to find a sample of students who would be most representative of the entire student body?

   (A) a math class

   (B) the cafeteria

   (C) the principal's office

   (D) the music room

Use a Sample
Statistics and Probability

DIRECTIONS: Read the information. Then, answer the questions.

Strategy   Use a random sample to make inferences about an entire population.

1. The data in the table was collected from two random samples of 100 students regarding students' school lunch preference. What inferences can be made based on the results?

	Hamburgers	Pizza	Hot Dogs	Total
Sample 1	20	64	16	100
Sample 2	14	68	18	100

It can be inferred that _____ is the first choice for school lunch.

Do students have much of a preference between hamburgers and hot dogs? Write how you know.

_____

_____

_____

_____

_____

_____

2. About how many slices of pizza should the school cafeteria prepare to serve 500 students?

   Ⓐ 250

   Ⓑ 330

   Ⓒ 400

   Ⓓ 500

3. Ben is ordering T-shirts for the school store. He surveyed and collected random samples of 100 students regarding student color preferences. Make at least two inferences based on the results.

	Yellow	White	Blue	Total
Sample 1	32	20	48	100
Sample 2	28	15	57	100

_____

_____

_____

_____

_____

_____

_____

4. Andrew is planning what to buy for his store downtown. He collected two random samples of 100 women regarding their preference. Choose all inferences that apply.

	Capris	Shorts	Pants	Total
Sample 1	59	16	25	100
Sample 2	49	23	28	100

   Ⓐ More than twice as many women prefer capris to shorts.

   Ⓑ More women prefer shorts than capris.

   Ⓒ Shorts and pants are about tied.

   Ⓓ Most women prefer capris.

Find the Mean, Median, and Mode
Statistics and Probability

Strategy Use the definitions of mean, median, and mode to compute them from a given data set.

Test Tip Always start by ordering the data from least to greatest.

DIRECTIONS: Use the following data set to answer questions 1–3.

8, 5, 8, 8, 10, 13, 17, 17, 25, 20, 7, 9.

1. What is the mean of the data?
   - (A) 8
   - (B) 9.5
   - (C) 12.25
   - (D) 20

2. What is the median of the data?
   - (A) 8
   - (B) 9.5
   - (C) 12.25
   - (D) 20

3. What is the mode of the data?
   - (A) 8
   - (B) 9.5
   - (C) 12.5
   - (D) There is no mode.

DIRECTIONS: Use the following data set for questions 4–7.

The basketball attendance per game for the season was: 80, 100, 60, 120, 120, 100, 140.

4. What is the mean of the data?

   _____

5. What is the median of the data?

   _____

Test Tip Remember that there can be more than one mode for a data set.

6. What is the mode of the data?

   _____

7. Suppose there had been an additional basketball game in the season. Attendance at this game was 100. How would this affect the mean, mode, and median of the data set?

   _____

   _____

   _____

   _____

Interpret Stem-and-Leaf Plots
Statistics and Probability

DIRECTIONS: Read the information. Then, answer the questions.

Strategy — Use data to make and interpret a stem-and-leaf plot.

1. Becca recorded the heights (in inches) of the students in her art class in a stem-and-leaf plot.

4	8 9
5	0 3 7 7 9
6	1 2 2 4 6

Key: 5 | 3 means 53

How many students are in the art class?

_____

How tall is the tallest person in the class?

_____

2. Elizabeth recorded her bowling scores in a stem-and-leaf plot.

9	7
10	0 2 7 8 9
11	1 3 3 4 6
12	0 5 8
13	2 4 6 9

Key: 12 | 5 means 125

What is Elizabeth's best score? _____

What is the mode of Elizabeth's bowling scores?

_____

Test Tip

Remember to make a key when you make a stem-and-leaf plot.

3. Your class just took a math test. These are the scores: 97, 99, 81, 78, 73, 95, 63, 97, 64, 100, 85, 83, 85, 88, 79, 80, 93, 82, 85, and 71. Make a stem-and-leaf plot of the data.

What is the range of the test scores? Show your work.

What is the mode of the test scores? _____

What is the median of the test scores? Write how you know.

_____

_____

Interpret Box-and-Whisker Plots

Statistics and Probability

DIRECTIONS: The box-and-whisker plot shows the number of volunteer hours performed by the students in Ms. Becker's homeroom last year. Use the box-and-whisker plot to answer the questions.

Strategy Use box-and-whisker plots to interpret data sets.

Test Tip Box-and-whisker plots identify the lower and upper extremes, the first and third quartiles, and the median.

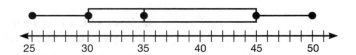

1. What is the median number of volunteer hours?

- (A) 25
- (B) 30
- (C) 35
- (D) 45

2. What is the first quartile of the data set?

- (A) 25
- (B) 30
- (C) 35
- (D) 45

3. What statement is not true about the box and whisker plot shown?

- (A) 15 represents the range of volunteer hours.
- (B) 45 represents the third quartile.
- (C) 50 represents the maximum number of volunteer hours performed.
- (D) Exactly half the items in the data are greater than the median.

4. What percentage of the data is between the first quartile and third quartile?

_____

5. Which of the following can be determined from a box and whisker plot?

- (A) the mean of a data set
- (B) the mode of a data set
- (C) the number of data points in a data set
- (D) the highest and lowest values in a data set

Use Simple Probability
Statistics and Probability

DIRECTIONS: Read the information. Then, answer the questions.

Strategy Understand that the probability of an event is a number between 0 and 1 that expresses the likelihood of the event occurring and use a probability model to determine probability of events.

Test Tip Remember the probability model:
$$\frac{\text{number of ways an event can occur}}{\text{number of possible outcomes}}$$

1. A candy jar has 4 green lollipops, 3 red lollipops, and 2 purple lollipops. A lollipop is drawn at random.

Do you think the probability of choosing a purple lollipop is closer to 0 or 1? Write how you know.

_____

Determine the probability of choosing a purple lollipop:

The number of ways a purple lollipop can be drawn is _____ .

The number of possible outcomes is

_____ + _____ + _____ = _____

$\dfrac{\text{number of ways event can occur}}{\text{number of possible outcomes}} = \dfrac{\boxed{}}{\boxed{}}$

2. Lionel rolls a number cube with the numbers 1 to 6. What is the probability of rolling a 4?

Rolling a 4 can occur _____ way. There are _____ possible outcomes. They are

_____

$\dfrac{\text{number of ways event can occur}}{\text{number of possible outcomes}} = \dfrac{\boxed{}}{\boxed{}}$

What is the probability of not rolling a 4?

The number of ways a number other than 4 can be rolled are _____

$\dfrac{\text{number of ways event can occur}}{\text{number of possible outcomes}} = \dfrac{\boxed{}}{\boxed{}}$

3. A jar contains 4 red marbles, 6 white marbles, and 5 blue marbles. If one marble is drawn at random, what is the probability that the marble is green?

(A) 0

(B) $\frac{1}{3}$

(C) $\frac{2}{5}$

(D) 1

4. What is the probability of selecting a vowel if a letter is chosen at random from the word **TRIANGLE**?

(A) $\frac{1}{4}$

(B) $\frac{3}{8}$

(C) $\frac{1}{2}$

(D) $\frac{5}{8}$

Use Experimental Probability
Statistics and Probability

DIRECTIONS: Read the information. Then, answer the questions.

Strategy Estimate the probability of an event by comparing the number of times the event occurs to the total number of trials.

Test Tip Remember the experimental probability model:

$$\frac{\text{frequency of event}}{\text{total number of trials}}$$

1. Jack has a bag of marbles. Jack pulls one marble from the bag 50 times. Each time he records the color of the marble that is drawn as shown in the table. He replaces the marble into the bag before he pulls the next one.

Color of Marble	Red	Blue	Green	Yellow
Frequency	11	14	12	13

The experimental probability for red is $\dfrac{\boxed{}}{50}$.

The experimental probability for blue is

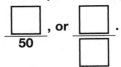 , or 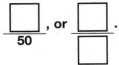 .

The experimental probability for green is

$\dfrac{\boxed{}}{50}$, or $\dfrac{\boxed{}}{\boxed{}}$.

The experimental probability for yellow is $\dfrac{\boxed{}}{50}$.

If Jack continues pulling marbles from the bag 1,000 times, how many times would he expect to pull a red marble?

Multiply the experimental probability for red by the number of trials.

$\frac{11}{50} \times 1{,}000 =$ _____

2. A number cube is tossed 40 times. The results are in the table below.

Number	1	2	3	4	5	6
Frequency	7	6	10	5	4	8

If the number cube is tossed 200 times, how many times would you expect to roll the number 1?

(A) 5

(B) 7

(C) 35

(D) 40

3. A restaurant records the ice cream flavors that its customers order for dessert. So far, vanilla was ordered by 14 customers, chocolate by 17 customers, strawberry by 21 customers, and butter pecan by 13 customers. What is the probability that the next customer orders butter pecan ice cream?

(A) $\frac{1}{65}$

(B) $\frac{1}{4}$

(C) $\frac{4}{5}$

(D) $\frac{1}{5}$

Use Compound Probability
Statistics and Probability

DIRECTIONS: Read the information. Then, answer the questions.

Strategy | Use organized lists, tables, and tree diagrams to find probabilities of compound events.

Test Tip | Lists, tables, and tree diagrams can be used to find the number of possible outcomes in a sample space.

1. Amelie is buying a new car. She can choose a black, silver, or white car. She may also choose leather or fabric seats. Make a tree diagram to find the sample space.

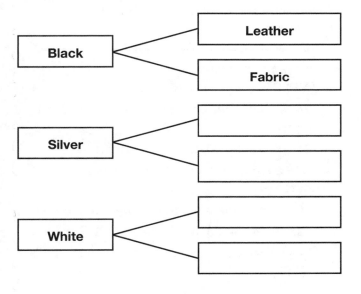

How many possible outcomes are there in the sample space? _____

Explain how the tree diagram shows the possible outcomes.

_____

_____

_____

What is the probability that Amelie buys a white car with leather seats? _____

2. Derek rolls 2 number cubes with the numbers 1 to 6. Make a table to find the sample space of rolling a particular sum with the number cubes.

	1	2	3	4	5	6
1	2	3	4	5	6	7
2						
3						
4						
5						
6						

How many possible outcomes are there in the sample space? _____

Find the probability that the sum of the numbers rolled is 7.

There are _____ ways to roll a 7.

The probability that the sum of the numbers rolled is 7 is _____ .

3. Alex rolls two number cubes. Find the probability that the sum of the numbers he rolls is 9 or greater.

   (A) $\frac{1}{10}$

   (B) $\frac{9}{10}$

   (C) $\frac{5}{18}$

   (D) $\frac{1}{2}$

Strategy Review

DIRECTIONS: Answer the questions.

Strategy
Apply prior knowledge and basic operations to solve problems.

EXAMPLE

A ticket to a play costs $30. There is a 5% transaction fee. What is the total cost of the ticket?

First, write the transaction fee percent as a decimal using what you know about percents.

5% = 0.05

Next, use multiplication. Multiply the cost of the ticket by the decimal.

$30 × 0.05 = $1.50

Next, use addition. Add the transaction fee to the cost of the ticket.

$30 + $1.50 = $31.50

The total cost of the ticket is $31.50.

1. Lucinda borrows $600 on a 3-year loan. She is charged 4% simple interest per year. What is the total amount Lucinda has to pay back?
   - (A) $72
   - (B) $624
   - (C) $672
   - (D) $1,800

2. The price of a pair of shoes is reduced from $40 to $32. What is the percent decrease?
   - (A) 8%
   - (B) 20%
   - (C) 25%
   - (D) 32%

How did the strategy help you answer these questions?

_____

_____

Strategy
Organize and display data in order to interpret it.

EXAMPLE

People on a nature walk have the following ages:

21, 14, 32, 14, 30, 25, 20, 14, 13, 21

Use a stem-and-leaf plot to organize the data.

First, order the ages from lowest to highest.

13, 14, 14, 14, 20, 21, 21, 25, 30, 32

Then, make a stem-and-leaf plot.

1	3 4 4 4
2	0 1 1 5
3	0 2

Key: 1│3 means 13

Now, you can use your stem-and-leaf plot to answer questions about the data.

3. **How many people went on the nature walk?** _____

4. **What is the mode of the data set?** _____

Strategy Review

Strategy   Look for key words in word problems that help you know which operation to use.

EXAMPLE

A game show contestant has 50 points. He answers a question correctly to win 15 points. Then, he answers 3 questions incorrectly and loses 25 points each time. What is the contestant's final score?

First, identify key words that tell you what operations to use.

The words "win 15 points" suggest addition.

The words "loses 25 points" suggest subtraction.

The words "each time" suggest multiplication.

Then, write an expression to represent the situation.

50 + 15 − 3(25)

Perform all multiplications and divisions, working from left to right. Separate each calculation as needed.

50 + 15 − 3(25) = 50 + 15 − 75

Continue performing operations working from left to right.

50 + 15 − 75 = 65 − 75 = −10

The contestant's final score is −10.

Strategy

Use drawings, graphs, or number lines to understand and solve a problem.

EXAMPLE

The temperature in Tannerville is −4°F. The temperature in Albion is 3 degrees less. What is the temperature in Albion?

First, draw a number line and plot the temperature in Tannerville.

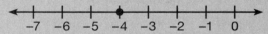

Then, move 3 tick marks to the left to show that the temperature in Albion is 3 degrees less.

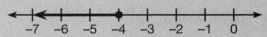

The temperature in Albion is −7°F.

2. A diver at 67 feet below the surface rises 10 feet. She then rises another 22 feet. She then moves 10 feet deeper. How many feet below the water's surface is the diver now? Make a drawing that helps you solve the problem.

1. In a football game in the first 5 plays, the Falcons gained 2 yards, lost 8 yards, gained 3 yards, lost 2 yards, and then lost 5 yards. What was the average gain or loss for the 5 plays?

Ⓐ 4 yards

Ⓑ −2 yards

Ⓒ −5 yards

Ⓓ −10 yards

Strategy Review

Strategy   Write and solve an equation to solve a real-world problem.

EXAMPLE

Julia spent $38 for shoes. This was $14 more than twice the cost of the belt she bought. How much was the belt?

First, write an equation that represents the situation or the problem.

Use b to represent the cost of the belt. The shoes cost $14 more than twice the cost of the belt.

So, the equation is
$38 = 14 + 2b$, or $2b + 14 = 38$.

Next, solve the equation for b.

$$2b + 14 = 38$$
$$2b + 14 - 14 = 38 - 14$$

Subtract 14 from both sides of the equation.

$$2b = 24$$
$$\frac{2b}{2} = \frac{24}{2}$$

Divide both sides by 2.

$$b = 12$$

The belt cost $12.

Strategy

Read word problems carefully to identify the given information and what you are being asked to find.

EXAMPLE

Tanya collects coins and stamps. She traded 3 less than one-half of her coins for some stamps. She has 17 coins now. She wants to collect 17 more by the end of the month. How many coins did Tanya start with?

What is the given information?
Tanya traded 3 less than one-half of her coins. She has 17 coins now. She wants to collect 17 more.

What are you being asked to find?
the number of coins she started with

1. **Pedro works 7 hours less than twice the number of hours that Gina works each week. If Pedro works 35 hours, how many hours does Gina work?**

   (A) 70

   (B) 28

   (C) 21

   (D) 14

2. **Bryan's mother is 5 years younger than 4 times the age of Bryan. If Bryan's mother is 39, how old is Bryan?**

   (A) 7

   (B) $8\frac{1}{2}$

   (C) 11

   (D) $11\frac{1}{2}$

3. **159 students and teachers went on a field trip to the zoo. They left at 9:00 A.M. There were 3 buses and all were filled. 6 students had to travel in a van. How many people were in each bus?**

   What is the given information?

   _____

   _____

   What are you being asked to find?

   _____

   Is any of the given information extra, or not needed?

   _____

Strategy Review

Strategy   Use rules, properties, or formulas to solve problems.

EXAMPLE

An online store uses shipping cartons that are 14 in. by 12 in. by 6 in. Use the formula for volume, $V = Bh$, to find the volume of the carton.

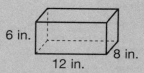

First, write the formula for the volume of a right rectangular prism.

$V = Bh$

Find the area of the base.

The base is a rectangle.
$A = lw = 12 \times 8 = 96$ in.^{2}

Use the volume formula.

$V = Bh = 96 \times 6 = 576$ in.^{3}

The volume of the carton is 576 in.^{3}

1. Find the surface area of the shipping carton in the example.

2. Garrett is making new seat cushions for his dining room chairs. The cushion is in the shape of a rectangular prism whose dimensions are 15 in. by 18 in. by 2 in. He is stuffing the cushions with foam. How much foam does he need for one cushion?

   (A) 336 in.^{3}

   (B) 540 in.^{3}

   (C) 672 in.^{3}

   (D) 1,080 in.^{3}

3. Garrett is covering each seat cushion with material. How much material is needed for one cushion?

   (A) 336 in.^{2}

   (B) 540 in.^{2}

   (C) 672 in.^{2}

   (D) 1,080 in.^{2}

Cite Text Evidence to Support Analysis
Reading: Literature

Strategy When reading, identify details that are clues to the setting, or the time and place in which this poem is set.

Test Tip To identify the setting, look for details about where the little rebel lives and why her relatives are fighting.

1. PART A: When does the action in this poem take place?
(A) during the French and Indian Wars
● during the American Revolution
(C) during Shays' Rebellion
(D) during the War of 1812

Part B: Which lines from the poem best support your answer to Part A? Choose three answers.
● ". . . With food to feed the people of the British-governed town;"
(B) "His apples and potatoes were fresh and fair and fine;"
● ". . . Who were fighting for the freedom that they meant to gain or die;"
(D) "But the treasures—how to get them?"
(E) " 'May I have a dozen apples for a kiss?' "
● ". . .Thought the little black-eyed rebel with a twinkle in her eye."

2. What effect does the poet create by ending each stanza with "her eye"?
Possible Answers: creates unity; the poet shows how the little rebel's feelings change throughout the poem; keeps the reader's attention on the central character

3. Which detail from the poem helps to clarify the meaning of *clinging*?
(A) The girl asks for a kiss.
(B) The boy was somewhat shy.
● The girl clasped her fingers.
(D) The boy's face flushed scarlet.

4. Which line shows how the girl feels in stanza 4?
"And a tear like silver glistened in the corner of her eye"

Write how you know. Why does she feel that way?
Possible Answer: She is thinking about the letters of soldiers that won't get to their loved ones. This makes her sad.

5. What problem does the little black-eyed rebel need to solve? Cite at least one line from the poem to support your answer.
The rebel needs to find a way to exchange letters with the boy without being caught by the British. Possible lines: "But the treasures—how to get them ... Since keen enemies were watching for what prizes they might find" and "Quick! the letters!" thrust them underneath my shawl! / Carry back again *this* package..."

Determine Theme
Reading: Literature

Strategy Focus on details related to what a character learns about life or how the character faces a problem in order to identify the theme of a story.

Test Tip To identify theme in this story, ask: *What lesson does Chris need to learn to solve his problem?*

1. What is the problem that Chris faces?
He is clumsy and feels awkward at team practice.

Write how you know.
She tells him, "Once you're used to your new body, you'll hardly remember how awkward you felt growing into it."

2. What do the words "slumping to the floor" tell you about Chris?
● He is discouraged.
(B) He is furious.
(C) He is proud.
(D) He is thrilled.

Write how you know.
The word *slumping* describes falling to the floor. Someone who slumps to the floor is sad or feels hopeless.

3. Why does Chris' grandmother insist on telling him a story?
(A) to help him accept his limitations
(B) to show him how to become a better athlete
● to encourage him to have patience with himself
(D) to teach him to treat others with more respect

4. Write the sentence that shows Chris doesn't believe he will get used to his new body as his grandmother says.
Possible Answer: " Yeah, right," said Chris with a skeptical expression.

5. Which character in the fable Chris' grandmother tells is most like Chris? Explain, using details from the story.
Possible Answer: The chrysalis is most like Chris, because their bodies are still growing. The chrysalis cannot move easily because it is still changing. Chris is also still changing as he grows.

Determine Theme
Reading: Literature

Strategy Combine the dialogue and words that tell what a character thinks or does to get a complete understanding of a character. Use that understanding to identify theme.

6. Which sentence below would make the best moral for the fable Chris' grandmother told?
(A) Beauty is only skin deep.
(B) Curiosity will lead you to many unexpected discoveries.
(C) Boast as much as you like as long as you can back up what you say.
● If you judge someone only by appearances, you will often be wrong.

7. What method does the author use to develop the theme of this story?
● A character tells a story within a story.
(B) Chris' grandmother explains cause-and-effect.
(C) A moral at the end of the fable sums up the lesson.
(D) The narrator moves between the present and the past.

Write how you know.
Possible Answer: The story states that Chris' grandmother tells a story: " 'Listen,' his grandmother said. 'I have a story to tell you.'"

Test Tip
Even when a question does not ask specifically for details from a story or passage, identify details and include them in your answer. The details support your answer.

8. What does Chris' grandmother want him to learn from the story of the chrysalis? Explain.
Possible Answer: She wants Chris to learn that if he is patient he will outgrow his clumsiness and grow into a better athlete. Supporting details may include the chrysalis difficulty in moving, the ant that boasts, and how easily the butterfly moves.

9. Will Chris' grandmother help Chris by telling the story? Explain your answer.
Possible Answer: Yes, because his grandmother has told stories before. I know this because in the story, Chris says "Not another story." Chris groaned, but he settled himself to listen." He complained about having to hear another story, but he "settled to listen." He will pay attention to what his grandmother says.

10. If Chris' grandmother is right, how will Chris play in future practices? Explain your answer.
Possible Answer: Chris will play well and not be awkward or clumsy. I know this because in Chris' grandmother's story, the caterpillar outgrew his awkwardness to become a graceful butterfly.

Analyze Interaction of Story Elements
Reading: Literature

Strategy To understand how story elements interact, ask yourself how the setting, characters, and events are all connected.

Test Tip To identify how the characters and the setting interact in "A New Tepee," ask how this story would be different if the characters lived in the same time and place as you.

1. Write details from the first paragraph that tell you about the setting of the story.
Possible Answer: Fingers of frost. It was a chilly autumn morning.

2. Why did Little Deer have "no time to snuggle beneath her buffalo skins"?
(A) She was going hunting with her brothers.
(B) She was mounting the lodge poles.
(C) She was making needles out of bone.
● She was sewing the cover of the tepee.

Write how you know.
Possible Answer: The story states: "It was going to be a busy day, helping her mother to finish the cover for their family's new tepee."

3. PART A: Why does Little Deer's family need a new tepee?
(A) to have a more beautiful tepee
(B) for protection from enemies
● to keep them warm in cold weather
(D) to replace one that does not have a cover

PART B: Write details from the story that you used to help you answer Part A.
Possible Answers: It is autumn. Little Deer's feet are cold. It is a chilly morning.

4. How does Little Deer's family use natural resources to survive on the Great Plains? Use at least three details from the story to support your answer.
Possible Answers: They use natural resources for food, shelter, clothing, and other needs. They use buffalo skins for clothing, blankets, and tepee coverings. They make tools from animal bone and rock. They use sinews for thread and rope. They trade for wooden lodge poles.

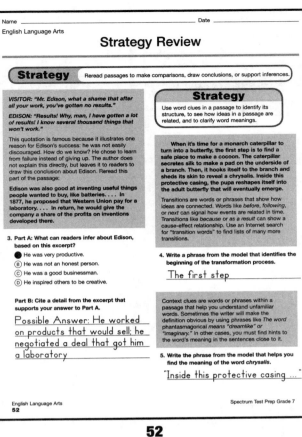

Page 52

Name _____ Date _____
English Language Arts

Strategy Review

Strategy — Reread passages to make comparisons, draw conclusions, or support inferences.

VISITOR: "Mr. Edison, what a shame that after all your work, you've gotten no results."

EDISON: "Results! Why, man, I have gotten a lot of results! I know several thousand things that won't work."

This quotation is famous because it illustrates one reason for Edison's success: he was not easily discouraged. How do we know? He chose to learn from failure instead of giving up. The author does not explain this directly, but leaves it to readers to draw this conclusion about Edison. Reread this part of the passage:

Edison was also good at inventing useful things people wanted to buy, like batteries. . . . In 1877, he proposed that Western Union pay for a laboratory. . . . In return, he would give the company a share of the profits on inventions developed there.

3. Part A: What can readers infer about Edison, based on this excerpt?

- ● He was very productive.
- Ⓑ He was not an honest person.
- Ⓒ He was a good businessman.
- Ⓓ He inspired others to be creative.

Part B: Cite a detail from the excerpt that supports your answer to Part A.

Possible Answer: He worked on products that would sell; he negotiated a deal that got him a laboratory

Strategy — Use word clues in a passage to identify its structure, to see how ideas in a passage are related, and to clarify word meanings.

When it's time for a monarch caterpillar to turn into a butterfly, the first step is to find a safe place to make a cocoon. The caterpillar secretes silk to make a pad on the underside of a branch. Then, it hooks itself to the branch and sheds its skin to reveal a chrysalis. Inside this protective casing, the pupa reshapes itself into the adult butterfly that will eventually emerge.

Transitions are words or phrases that show how ideas are connected. Words like before, following, or next can signal how events are related in time. Transitions like because or as a result can show a cause-effect relationship. Use an Internet search for "transition words" to find lists of many more transitions.

4. Write a phrase from the model that identifies the beginning of the transformation process.

The first step

Context clues are words or phrases within a passage that help you understand unfamiliar words. Sometimes the writer will make the definition obvious by using phrases like The word phantasmagorical means "dreamlike" or "imaginary." In other cases, you must find hints to the word's meaning in the sentences close to it.

5. Write the phrase from the model that helps you find the meaning of the word chrysalis.

"Inside this protective casing ... "

English Language Arts
52

Spectrum Test Prep Grade 7

52

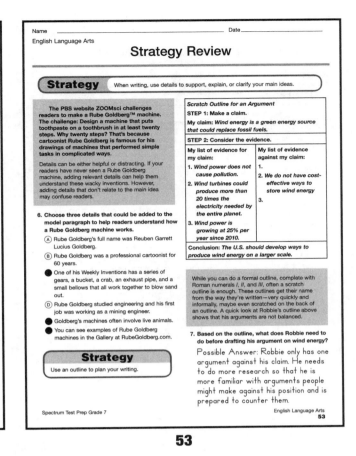

Page 53

Name _____ Date _____
English Language Arts

Strategy Review

Strategy — When writing, use details to support, explain, or clarify your main ideas.

The PBS website ZOOMsci challenges readers to make a Rube Goldberg™ machine. The challenge: Design a machine that puts toothpaste on a toothbrush in at least twenty steps. Why twenty steps? That's because cartoonist Rube Goldberg is famous for his drawings of machines that performed simple tasks in complicated ways.

Details can be either helpful or distracting. If your readers have never seen a Rube Goldberg machine, adding relevant details can help them understand these wacky inventions. However, adding details that don't relate to the main idea may confuse readers.

6. Choose three details that could be added to the model paragraph to help readers understand how a Rube Goldberg machine works.

- Ⓐ Rube Goldberg's full name was Reuben Garrett Lucius Goldberg.
- Ⓑ Rube Goldberg was a professional cartoonist for 60 years.
- ● One of his Weekly Inventions has a series of gears, a bucket, a crab, an exhaust pipe, and a small bellows that all work together to blow sand out.
- Ⓓ Rube Goldberg studied engineering and his first job was working as a mining engineer.
- ● Goldberg's machines often involve live animals.
- ● You can see examples of Rube Goldberg machines in the Gallery at RubeGoldberg.com.

Strategy — Use an outline to plan your writing.

Scratch Outline for an Argument

STEP 1: Make a claim.

My claim: Wind energy is a green energy source that could replace fossil fuels.

STEP 2: Consider the evidence.

My list of evidence for my claim:	My list of evidence against my claim:
1. Wind power does not cause pollution.	1.
2. Wind turbines could produce more than 20 times the electricity needed by the entire planet.	2. We do not have cost-effective ways to store wind energy
3. Wind power is growing at 25% per year since 2010.	

Conclusion: The U.S. should develop ways to produce wind energy on a larger scale.

While you can do a formal outline, complete with Roman numerals I, II, and III, often a scratch outline is enough. These outlines get their name from the way they're written—very quickly and informally, maybe even scratched on the back of an outline. A quick look at Robbie's outline above shows that his arguments are not balanced.

7. Based on the outline, what does Robbie need to do before drafting his argument on wind energy?

Possible Answer: Robbie only has one argument against his claim. He needs to do more research so that he is more familiar with arguments people might make against his position and is prepared to counter them.

Spectrum Test Prep Grade 7

English Language Arts
53

53

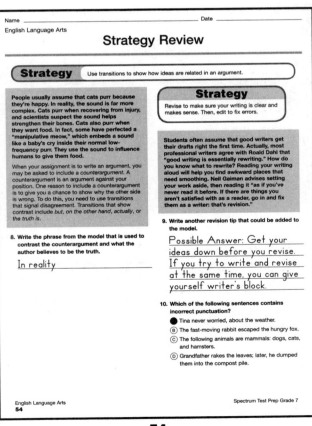

Page 54

Name _____ Date _____
English Language Arts

Strategy Review

Strategy — Use transitions to show how ideas are related in an argument.

People usually assume that cats purr because they're happy. In reality, the sound is far more complex. Cats purr when recovering from injury, and scientists suspect the sound helps strengthen their bones. Cats also purr when they want food. In fact, some have perfected a "manipulative meow," which embeds a sound like a baby's cry inside their normal low-frequency purr. They use the sound to influence humans to give them food.

When your assignment is to write an argument, you may be asked to include a counterargument. A counterargument is an argument against your position. One reason to include a counterargument is to give you a chance to show why the other side is wrong. To do this, you need to use transitions that signal disagreement. Transitions that show contrast include but, on the other hand, actually, or the truth is.

8. Write the phrase from the model that is used to contrast the counterargument and what the author believes to be the truth.

In reality

Strategy — Revise to make sure your writing is clear and makes sense. Then, edit to fix errors.

Students often assume that good writers get their drafts right the first time. Actually, most professional writers agree with Roald Dahl. "good writing is essentially rewriting." How do you know what to rewrite? Reading your writing aloud will help you find awkward places that need smoothing. Neil Gaiman advises setting your work aside, then reading it "as if you've never read it before. If there are things you aren't satisfied with as a reader, go in and fix them as a writer: that's revision."

9. Write another revision tip that could be added to the model.

Possible Answer: Get your ideas down before you revise. If you try to write and revise at the same time, you can give yourself writer's block.

10. Which of the following sentences contains incorrect punctuation?

- ● Tina never worried, about the weather.
- Ⓑ The fast-moving rabbit escaped the hungry fox.
- Ⓒ The following animals are mammals: dogs, cats, and hamsters.
- Ⓓ Grandfather rakes the leaves; later, he dumped them into the compost pile.

English Language Arts
54

Spectrum Test Prep Grade 7

54

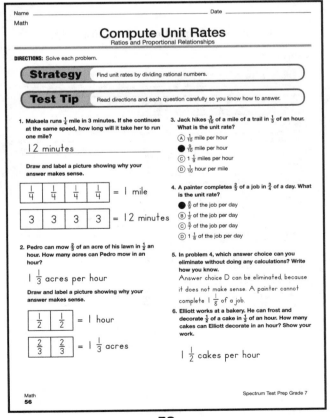

Page 56

Name _____ Date _____
Math

Compute Unit Rates
Ratios and Proportional Relationships

DIRECTIONS: Solve each problem.

Strategy — Find unit rates by dividing rational numbers.

Test Tip — Read directions and each question carefully so you know how to answer.

1. Makaela runs $\frac{1}{4}$ mile in 3 minutes. If she continues at the same speed, how long will it take her to run one mile?

12 minutes

Draw and label a picture showing why your answer makes sense.

| $\frac{1}{4}$ | $\frac{1}{4}$ | $\frac{1}{4}$ | $\frac{1}{4}$ | = 1 mile |

| 3 | 3 | 3 | 3 | = 12 minutes |

2. Pedro can mow $\frac{2}{3}$ of an acre of his lawn in $\frac{1}{2}$ an hour. How many acres can Pedro mow in an hour?

$1\frac{1}{3}$ acres per hour

Draw and label a picture showing why your answer makes sense.

| $\frac{1}{2}$ | $\frac{1}{2}$ | = 1 hour |

| $\frac{2}{3}$ | $\frac{2}{3}$ | = $1\frac{1}{3}$ acres |

3. Jack hikes $\frac{3}{10}$ of a mile of a trail in $\frac{1}{3}$ of an hour. What is the unit rate?

- Ⓐ $\frac{1}{10}$ mile per hour
- ● $\frac{9}{10}$ mile per hour
- Ⓒ $1\frac{1}{10}$ miles per hour
- Ⓓ $\frac{1}{10}$ hour per mile

4. A painter completes $\frac{2}{3}$ of a job in $\frac{3}{4}$ of a day. What is the unit rate?

- ● $\frac{8}{9}$ of the job per day
- Ⓑ $\frac{1}{2}$ of the job per day
- Ⓒ $\frac{9}{2}$ of the job per day
- Ⓓ $1\frac{1}{8}$ of the job per day

5. In problem 4, which answer choice can you eliminate without doing any calculations? Write how you know.

Answer choice D can be eliminated, because it does not make sense. A painter cannot complete $1\frac{1}{8}$ of a job.

6. Elliott works at a bakery. He can frost and decorate $\frac{1}{2}$ of a cake in $\frac{1}{3}$ of an hour. How many cakes can Elliott decorate in an hour? Show your work.

$1\frac{1}{2}$ cakes per hour

Math
56

Spectrum Test Prep Grade 7

56

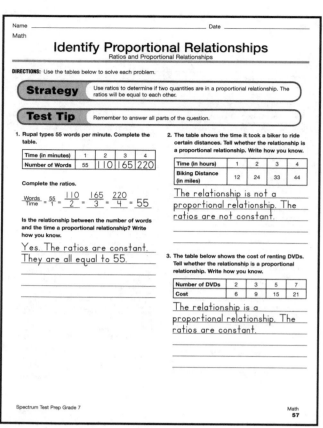

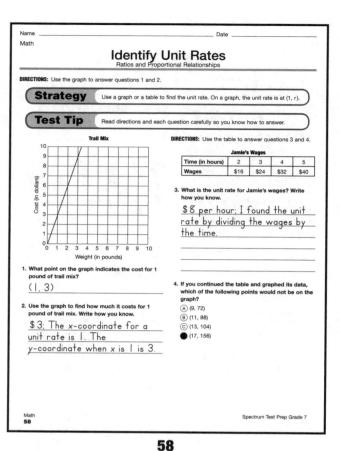

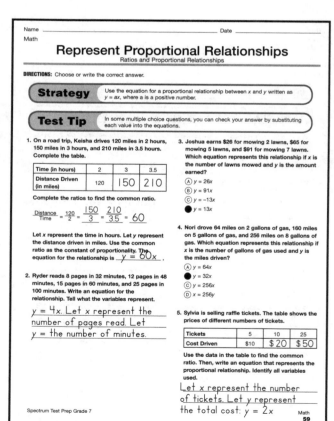

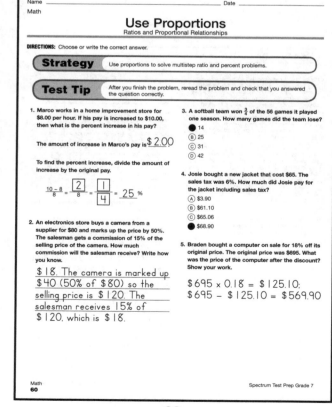

Absolute Value and Opposite Integers
The Number System

DIRECTIONS: Choose or write the correct answer.

Strategy — Identify opposite integers as integers whose absolute values are the same and whose sum is 0.

1. Use the number line to answer the questions.

-10 -9 -8 -7 -6 -5 -4 -3 -2 -1 0 1 2 3 4 5 6 7 8 9 10

How far is 6 from 0 and in which direction?

6 units to the right

What is the opposite of 6?

−6

How far is −6 from 0 and in which direction?

6 units to the left

The sum of 6 and its opposite, −6, is __0__ ,

Test Tip — The absolute value of a number is the number of units it is from 0 on the number line. The absolute value of a number n is written as $|n|$.

2. Write an integer to describe each situation. Then, give the situation and integer that describes the opposite situation. Finally, write the absolute value of the integer.

3 degrees below zero

Integer: __−3__

Situation, Opposite Integer:

3 degrees above zero, +3

Absolute Value: $|-3| = 3$

a gain of 8 yards in a football game

Integer: __+8__

Situation, Opposite Integer:

a loss of 8 yards, −8

Absolute Value: $|8| = 8$

3. Explain why a deposit of $20 and a withdrawal of $20 are opposite quantities.

If you deposit $20 and then withdraw $20, the transactions cancel each other out.

4. $|7| + |-8| =$ ☐

Ⓐ −1
Ⓑ −15
Ⓒ 1
● 15

5. $|25| =$ ☐

Ⓐ −25
● 25
Ⓒ 5
Ⓓ 50

6. Solve and show your work.

$|-9| + |7| - |5| \times |-2| =$ ☐ 6

$|-9| + |7| - |5| \times |-2|$
$= 9 + 7 - 5 \times 2$
$= 9 + 7 - 10 = 6$

61

Add and Subtract Integers
The Number System

DIRECTIONS: Choose or write the correct answer.

Strategy — Use number lines or rules to add and subtract integers.

Test Tip — Write down the rules for adding and subtracting integers before you start.

1. Garrett owes his friend Taylor $4. If he borrows another $3, how much will he owe Taylor altogether?

Owing $4 can be represented by __−4__ .

Owing $3 can be represented by __−3__ .

The problem can be solved by adding −4 + −3. Draw a number line from −10 to 10 and use it to find the sum.

Start at 0. Move __4__ to the left. Then, move 3 to the __left__ .

Since −4 + −3 = __−7__ , Garrett will owe Taylor __$7__ .

2. The temperature at noon was 8°F. By 6:00 P.M., the temperature had dropped 10°. What was the temperature at 6:00 P.M.?

Since 8 + (−10) = __−2__ , the temperature at 6:00 P.M. will be __−2°__ .

3. −6 + −2 = __−8__

4. 13 + (−9) = __4__

5. 12 − (−3) = ☐

Ⓐ −15
Ⓑ −9
Ⓒ 9
● 15

6. −7 + 7 = ☐

Ⓐ −14
● 0
Ⓒ 14
Ⓓ 49

7. Tobiah starts with $125.00 in her bank account. On Saturday, she withdraws $35.00 to buy books for school. On Monday, she deposits $20.00 in babysitting money. On Tuesday, the bank charges her a $3 monthly fee. How much money is in her account at the end of Tuesday? Show your work.

$125 − $35 + $20 − $3 =
$90 + $20 − $3 =
$110 − $3 =
$107

There is $107 in her account.

62

Add and Subtract Rational Numbers
The Number System

DIRECTIONS: Choose or write the correct answer.

Strategy — Extend rules for adding and subtracting integers to all rational numbers.

Test Tip — Remember that you can rewrite a subtraction expression as an addition expression: 4.6 − (−0.8) = 4.6 + (0.8).

1. Find $2\frac{3}{4} + 1\frac{2}{3}$.

$4\frac{5}{12}$

Explain how you found your answer.

Possible Answer: First, I converted the mixed numbers to improper fractions. Then, I added the fractions. Then, I simplified.

2. Find 4.58 + (−6.25) − (−1.67). Show your work.

0; 4.58 + (−6.25) − (−1.67)
= 4.58 − 6.25 + 1.67
= 0

3. $-\frac{2}{3} + 4\frac{1}{6} =$ ☐

● $3\frac{1}{2}$
Ⓑ $4\frac{5}{6}$
Ⓒ $-3\frac{1}{2}$
Ⓓ $-4\frac{5}{6}$

4. 6.07 − (−3.94) = ☐

Ⓐ −2.13
Ⓑ 2.13
Ⓒ −10.01
● 10.01

63

Use Properties
The Number System

DIRECTIONS: Choose or write the correct answer.

Strategy — Apply properties of operations as strategies to perform operations with rational numbers.

Test Tip — The **commutative property** says you can switch the order of the numbers and still get the same answer. The **associative property** says you can change the grouping of the numbers and still get the same answer. The **distributive property** is used when there is a combination of multiplication over addition or subtraction.

1. Simplify $-4\frac{5}{8} + 3.2 - \frac{1}{8}$.

$-4\frac{5}{8} + 3.2 - \frac{1}{8}$

$= -4\frac{5}{8} + 3.2 + (-\frac{1}{8})$ since subtracting a number is the same as adding its __opposite__ .

$= -4\frac{5}{8} + (-\frac{1}{8}) + 3.2$ by the __Commutative__ Property of Addition.

$= (-4\frac{5}{8} + (-\frac{1}{8})) + 3.2$ by the __Associative__ Property of Addition.

$= $ __−5__ $ + 3.2$

$= $ __−1.8__

DIRECTIONS: For questions 2–3, use the properties of operations to evaluate each expression.

2. $7.8 - 2\frac{7}{8} - (-3.2)$

$8\frac{1}{8}$

What property did you use to evaluate the expression?

Commutative

3. $6(4\frac{2}{3} - 2\frac{1}{2})$

__13__

What property did you use to evaluate the expression?

Distributive

4. Shar uses the Associative Property to help her evaluate the expression $9 - (8 + \frac{1}{3}) + \frac{2}{3}$. Which expression did she evaluate?

Ⓐ $9 + (8 + \frac{1}{3} + \frac{2}{3})$
Ⓑ $9(8) + (\frac{1}{3} + \frac{2}{3})$
● $(9 - 8) + (\frac{1}{3} + \frac{2}{3})$
Ⓓ $\frac{2}{3} + 9 + \frac{1}{3} - 8$

64

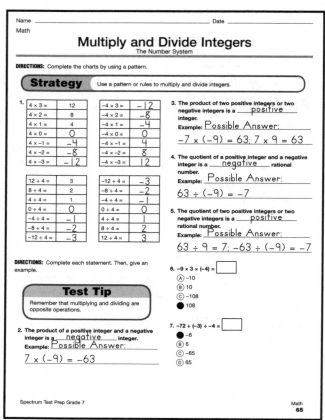

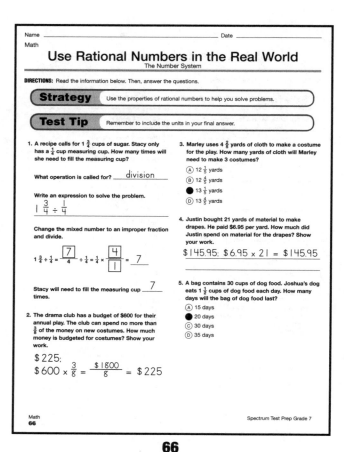

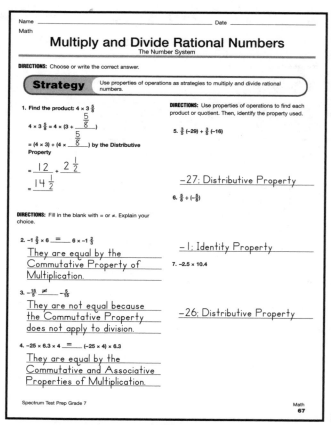

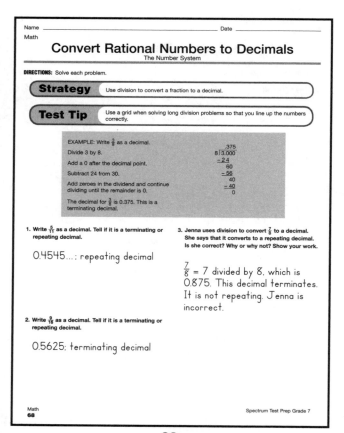

65

66

67

68

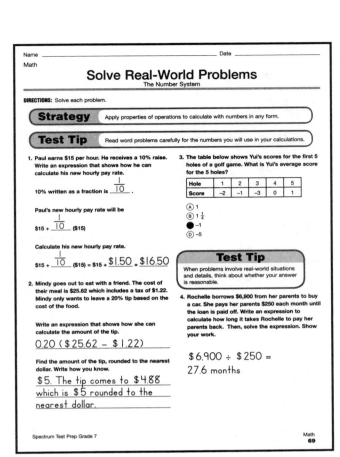

Solve Real-World Problems
The Number System

DIRECTIONS: Solve each problem.

Strategy Apply properties of operations to calculate with numbers in any form.

Test Tip Read word problems carefully for the numbers you will use in your calculations.

1. Paul earns $15 per hour. He receives a 10% raise. Write an expression that shows how he can calculate his new hourly pay rate.

10% written as a fraction is $\frac{1}{10}$.

Paul's new hourly pay rate will be

$15 + $\frac{1}{10}$ ($15)

Calculate his new hourly pay rate.

$15 + $\frac{1}{10}$ ($15) = $15 + $1.50 = $16.50

2. Mindy goes out to eat with a friend. The cost of their meal is $25.62 which includes a tax of $1.22. Mindy only wants to leave a 20% tip based on the cost of the food.

Write an expression that shows how she can calculate the amount of the tip.

$0.20 ($25.62 - $1.22)$

Find the amount of the tip, rounded to the nearest dollar. Write how you know.

$5. The tip comes to $4.88 which is $5 rounded to the nearest dollar.

3. The table below shows Yui's scores for the first 5 holes of a golf game. What is Yui's average score for the 5 holes?

Hole	1	2	3	4	5
Score	-2	-1	-3	0	1

Ⓐ 1
Ⓑ 1 $\frac{1}{4}$
● -1
Ⓓ -5

Test Tip
When problems involve real-world situations and details, think about whether your answer is reasonable.

4. Rochelle borrows $6,900 from her parents to buy a car. She pays her parents $250 each month until the loan is paid off. Write an expression to calculate how long it takes Rochelle to pay her parents back. Then, solve the expression. Show your work.

$6,900 ÷ $250 = 27.6 months

69

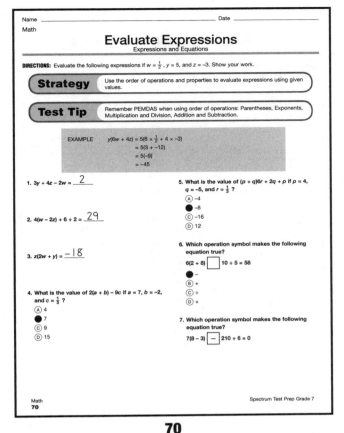

Evaluate Expressions
Expressions and Equations

DIRECTIONS: Evaluate the following expressions if $w = \frac{1}{2}$, $y = 5$, and $z = -3$. Show your work.

Strategy Use the order of operations and properties to evaluate expressions using given values.

Test Tip Remember PEMDAS when using order of operations: Parentheses, Exponents, Multiplication and Division, Addition and Subtraction.

EXAMPLE
$y(6w + 4z) = 5(6 \times \frac{1}{2} + 4 \times -3)$
$= 5(3 + -12)$
$= 5(-9)$
$= -45$

1. $3y + 4z - 2w =$ __2__

2. $4(w - 2z) + 6 \div 2 =$ __29__

3. $z(2w + y) =$ __-18__

4. What is the value of $2(a + b) - 9c$ if $a = 7$, $b = -2$, and $c = \frac{1}{3}$?
Ⓐ 4
● 7
Ⓒ 9
Ⓓ 15

5. What is the value of $(p + q)6r + 2q + p$ if $p = 4$, $q = -5$, and $r = \frac{1}{3}$?
Ⓐ -4
● -8
Ⓒ -16
Ⓓ 12

6. Which operation symbol makes the following equation true?

$6(2 + 8)$ ☐ $10 \div 5 = 58$

● -
Ⓑ +
Ⓒ ÷
Ⓓ ×

7. Which operation symbol makes the following equation true?

$7(8 - 3)$ ☐ $210 \div 6 = 0$

70

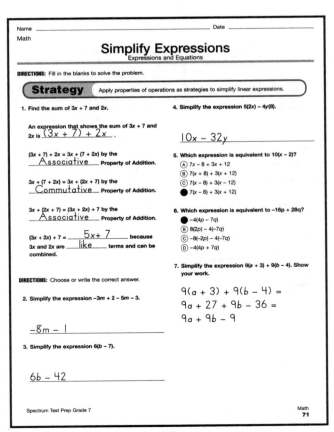

Simplify Expressions
Expressions and Equations

DIRECTIONS: Fill in the blanks to solve the problem.

Strategy Apply properties of operations as strategies to simplify linear expressions.

1. Find the sum of $3x + 7$ and $2x$.

An expression that shows the sum of $3x + 7$ and $2x$ is $(3x + 7) + 2x$

$(3x + 7) + 2x = 3x + (7 + 2x)$ by the __Associative__ Property of Addition.

$3x + (7 + 2x) = 3x + (2x + 7)$ by the __Commutative__ Property of Addition.

$3x + (2x + 7) = (3x + 2x) + 7$ by the __Associative__ Property of Addition.

$(3x + 2x) + 7 =$ __5x + 7__ because $3x$ and $2x$ are __like__ terms and can be combined.

DIRECTIONS: Choose or write the correct answer.

2. Simplify the expression $-3m + 2 - 5m - 3$.

__-8m - 1__

3. Simplify the expression $6(b - 7)$.

__6b - 42__

4. Simplify the expression $5(2x) - 4y(8)$.

__10x - 32y__

5. Which expression is equivalent to $10(x - 2)$?
Ⓐ $7x - 8 + 3x + 12$
Ⓑ $7(x + 8) + 3(x + 12)$
Ⓒ $7(x - 8) + 3(x - 12)$
● $7(x - 8) + 3(x + 12)$

6. Which expression is equivalent to $-16p + 28q$?
● $-4(4p - 7q)$
Ⓑ $8(2p) - 4(-7q)$
Ⓒ $-8(-2p) - 4(-7q)$
Ⓓ $-4(4p + 7q)$

7. Simplify the expression $9(a + 3) + 9(b - 4)$. Show your work.

$9(a + 3) + 9(b - 4) =$
$9a + 27 + 9b - 36 =$
$9a + 9b - 9$

71

Rewrite Expressions
Expressions and Equations

DIRECTIONS: Read the information below. Then, complete the statements.

Strategy Rewrite an expression in different forms to show how the quantities in it are related.

Test Tip Look for key words to help you solve a word problem. If someone gets a raise in wages, the new rate will be greater than the old one. If something is on sale, its new price will be less than the old price.

1. Sydney is getting a 3% raise to her hourly pay. Write an expression that represents her new hourly pay rate.

Sydney's hourly pay rate will increase by __3__ %, which is __0.03__ written in decimal form.

If Sydney's current hourly pay is h, then her new hourly pay will be $h +$ __0.03h__ .

$h + 0.03h = 1h + 0.03h =$ __1.03h__

DIRECTIONS: Choose or write the correct answer.

2. A bike store is having a 20% off sale. Write an expression that represents the cost of buying a bike that is on sale at the store.

__0.8b__

3. A camera store marks up the cost of a camera by 35%. Which expression represents the price that the camera sells for?
Ⓐ $0.35c$
● $1.35c$
Ⓒ $35c$
Ⓓ $\frac{c}{35}$

4. Tell if the statement is true or false.

An increase by 15% is the same as multiplying by 1.15. __true__

A 25% discount is the same as finding 75% of the cost. __true__

A markup by 40% is the same as multiplying by 1.04. __false__

5. A department store offers 25% off any small appliance. Suzanne has a coupon for $5 off any purchase. If a coffee maker normally sells for $45, write an expression that represents how much will it cost Suzanne after both the sale discount and the coupon.

$$45(0.75) - 5
$(45 - 5) \times 0.75$

72

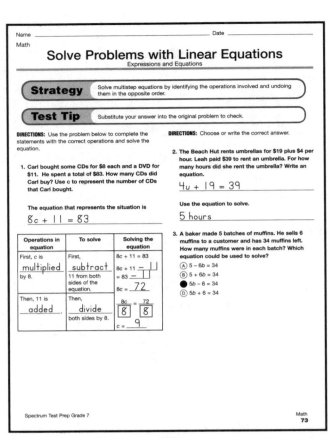

73

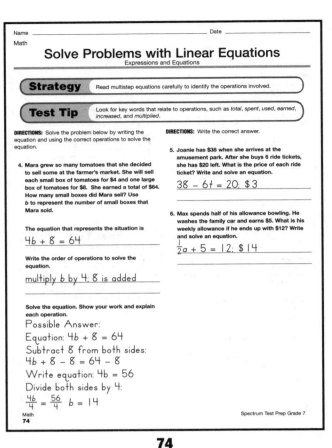

74

Page 73

Solve Problems with Linear Equations
Expressions and Equations

Strategy Solve multistep equations by identifying the operations involved and undoing them in the opposite order.

Test Tip Substitute your answer into the original problem to check.

DIRECTIONS: Use the problem below to complete the statements with the correct operations and solve the equation.

1. Carl bought some CDs for $8 each and a DVD for $11. He spent a total of $83. How many CDs did Carl buy? Use c to represent the number of CDs that Carl bought.

The equation that represents the situation is

$8c + 11 = 83$

Operations in equation	To solve	Solving the equation
First, c is **multiplied** by 8.	First, **subtract** 11 from both sides of the equation.	$8c + 11 = 83$ $8c + 11 - 11 = 83 - 11$ $8c = 72$
Then, 11 is **added**.	Then, **divide** both sides by 8.	$\frac{8c}{8} = \frac{72}{8}$ $c = 9$

DIRECTIONS: Choose or write the correct answer.

2. The Beach Hut rents umbrellas for $19 plus $4 per hour. Leah paid $39 to rent an umbrella. For how many hours did she rent the umbrella? Write an equation.

$4u + 19 = 39$

Use the equation to solve.

5 hours

3. A baker made 5 batches of muffins. He sells 6 muffins to a customer and has 34 muffins left. How many muffins were in each batch? Which equation could be used to solve?

Ⓐ $5 - 6b = 34$
Ⓑ $5 + 6b = 34$
● $5b - 6 = 34$
Ⓓ $5b + 6 = 34$

Page 74

Solve Problems with Linear Equations
Expressions and Equations

Strategy Read multistep equations carefully to identify the operations involved.

Test Tip Look for key words that relate to operations, such as *total, spent, used, earned, increased,* and *multiplied*.

DIRECTIONS: Solve the problem below by writing the equation and using the correct operations to solve the equation.

4. Mara grew so many tomatoes that she decided to sell some at the farmer's market. She will sell each small box of tomatoes for $4 and one large box of tomatoes for $8. She earned a total of $64. How many small boxes did Mara sell? Use b to represent the number of small boxes that Mara sold.

The equation that represents the situation is

$4b + 8 = 64$

Write the order of operations to solve the equation.

multiply b by 4; 8 is added

Solve the equation. Show your work and explain each operation.

Possible Answer:
Equation: $4b + 8 = 64$
Subtract 8 from both sides:
$4b + 8 - 8 = 64 - 8$
Write equation: $4b = 56$
Divide both sides by 4:
$\frac{4b}{4} = \frac{56}{4}$ $b = 14$

DIRECTIONS: Write the correct answer.

5. Joanie has $38 when she arrives at the amusement park. After she buys 6 ride tickets, she has $20 left. What is the price of each ride ticket? Write and solve an equation.

$38 - 6t = 20; \$3$

6. Max spends half of his allowance bowling. He washes the family car and earns $5. What is his weekly allowance if he ends up with $12? Write and solve an equation.

$\frac{1}{2}a + 5 = 12; \$14$

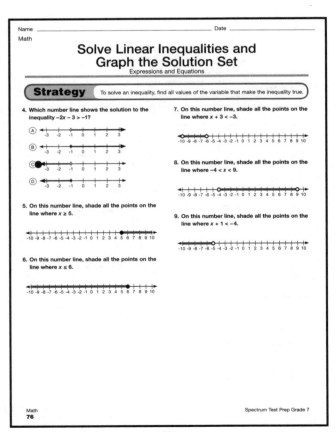

75

76

Page 75

Solve Linear Inequalities and Graph the Solution Set
Expressions and Equations

Strategy Write, solve, and graph an inequality and interpret the solution within the context of the problem.

Test Tip Remember to reverse the inequality sign when multiplying or dividing both sides of an inequality by a negative number.

1. Eloise needs $23 to buy a new calculator. Her mother agrees to pay her $5 an hour for cleaning up the basement in addition to her $8 weekly allowance. What is the minimum number of hours Eloise must work to have enough money to purchase the calculator?

Write an inequality to represent the situation.

$5h + 8 \geq 23$

Solve the inequality. $h \geq 3$

So, Eloise must work at least **3** hours.

Graph the solution to the inequality.

2. Tim will have his birthday party at the bowling alley with some friends, but the most he can spend is $75. The bowling alley charges a flat fee of $25 for a private party and $8 per person for shoe rentals and unlimited bowling. The birthday person bowls free. What is the greatest number of friends Tim can invite? Write and solve an inequality. Then, graph the solution.

$8p + 25 \leq 75; p \leq 6.25;$
Tim can invite 6 friends.

3. Caleb has $6. Rolls cost $0.80 each and a container of margarine costs $1.50. If Caleb buys one container of margarine, how many rolls can he buy? Write how you know.

Caleb can buy 5 rolls. I wrote and solved the inequality $0.8r + 1.50 \leq 6.00$. $r \leq 5.625$. Caleb cannot buy part of a roll.

Page 76

Solve Linear Inequalities and Graph the Solution Set
Expressions and Equations

Strategy To solve an inequality, find all values of the variable that make the inequality true.

4. Which number line shows the solution to the inequality $-2x - 3 > -1$?

Ⓐ
Ⓑ
● Ⓒ
Ⓓ

5. On this number line, shade all the points on the line where $x \geq 5$.

6. On this number line, shade all the points on the line where $x \leq 6$.

7. On this number line, shade all the points on the line where $x + 3 < -3$.

8. On this number line, shade all the points on the line where $-4 < x < 9$.

9. On this number line, shade all the points on the line where $x + 1 < -4$.

Scale Drawings
Geometry

DIRECTIONS: Complete the statements and solve the problem.

Strategy Use proportions to solve problems involving scale drawings of geometric figures.

1. Chris is building a rectangular deck. He makes a scale drawing of the deck. If each 2 cm on the scale drawing equals 5 ft., what are the actual dimensions of the deck?

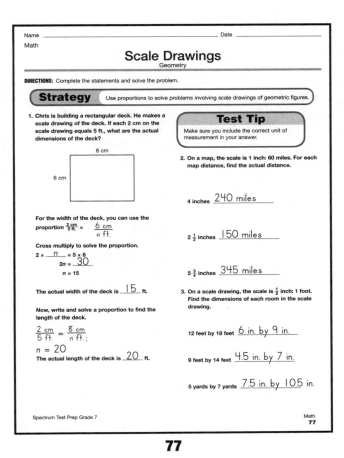

For the width of the deck, you can use the proportion $\frac{2\ cm}{5\ ft.}$ = $\frac{6\ cm}{n\ ft.}$

Cross multiply to solve the proportion.

$2 \times \underline{n} = 5 \times 6$

$2n = \underline{30}$

$n = 15$

The actual width of the deck is $\underline{15}$ ft.

Now, write and solve a proportion to find the length of the deck.

$\frac{2\ cm}{5\ ft.} = \frac{8\ cm}{n\ ft.}$;

$n = 20$

The actual length of the deck is $\underline{20}$ ft.

Test Tip

Make sure you include the correct unit of measurement in your answer.

2. On a map, the scale is 1 inch: 60 miles. For each map distance, find the actual distance.

4 inches $\underline{240\ miles}$

$2\frac{1}{2}$ inches $\underline{150\ miles}$

$5\frac{3}{4}$ inches $\underline{345\ miles}$

3. On a scale drawing, the scale is $\frac{1}{2}$ inch: 1 foot. Find the dimensions of each room in the scale drawing.

12 feet by 18 feet $\underline{6\ in.\ by\ 9\ in.}$

9 feet by 14 feet $\underline{4.5\ in.\ by\ 7\ in.}$

5 yards by 7 yards $\underline{7.5\ in.\ by\ 10.5\ in.}$

77

Scale Drawings
Geometry

DIRECTIONS: Use the figure to draw a new figure with a different scale.

Strategy Read all of the measurements of a scale drawing carefully. Then, reread the word problem and compare the measurements on the scale drawing to the numbers in the word problem.

4. In the scale drawing, assume the rectangle is drawn on centimeter grid paper. The scale is 1 cm: 2 m.

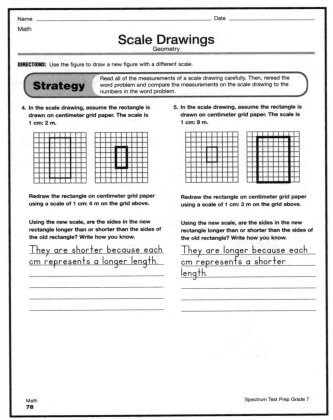

Redraw the rectangle on centimeter grid paper using a scale of 1 cm: 4 m on the grid above.

Using the new scale, are the sides in the new rectangle longer than or shorter than the sides of the old rectangle? Write how you know.

$\underline{They\ are\ shorter\ because\ each}$
$\underline{cm\ represents\ a\ longer\ length.}$

5. In the scale drawing, assume the rectangle is drawn on centimeter grid paper. The scale is 1 cm: 9 m.

Redraw the rectangle on centimeter grid paper using a scale of 1 cm: 3 m on the grid above.

Using the new scale, are the sides in the new rectangle longer than or shorter than the sides of the old rectangle? Write how you know.

$\underline{They\ are\ longer\ because\ each}$
$\underline{cm\ represents\ a\ shorter}$
$\underline{length.}$

78

Draw and Classify Figures
Geometry

DIRECTIONS: Use a ruler and a protractor to construct figures with the given conditions. Then, classify the figures.

Strategy Use the attributes of shapes and tools such as a protractor to draw geometric shapes with given conditions.

1. Follow the instructions below to construct triangle ABC with AB = 5 cm, ∠BAC = 30°, and ∠ABC = 70°.

Step 1: Draw and label a line segment AB that is 6 cm long.

Step 2: Use a protractor to draw an angle of 30° at point A.

Step 3: Use a protractor to draw an angle of 70° at point B.

Step 4: If necessary, extend the lines until they intersect each other at C to form triangle ABC.

Classify △ABC.

$\underline{acute\ scalene}$

2. △DEF with DE = 1 in., ∠EDF = 110°, and ∠DEF = 50°

Classify △DEF.

$\underline{obtuse\ scalene}$

3. △PQR with PQ = 7 cm, ∠QPR = 60°, and ∠PQR = 60°

Classify △PQR.

$\underline{right\ isosceles}$

79

Draw and Classify Figures
Geometry

DIRECTIONS: Use a ruler and a protractor to construct figures with the given conditions.

Strategy Use the given conditions when drawing angles, making sure you are using the conditions presented in the problem.

Test Tip Make sure you have a straight edge and protractor when you take a geometry test.

4. Follow the instructions below to construct triangle XYZ with XY = 8 cm, XZ = 7 cm and ∠ZXY = 60°.

Step 1: Draw and label a line segment XY that is 8 cm long.

Step 2: Mark an angle of 60° by placing the protractor at point X.

Step 3: Join the 60° mark and point X. Extend XZ until it is 7 cm long.

Step 4: Join points Y and Z to complete the triangle.

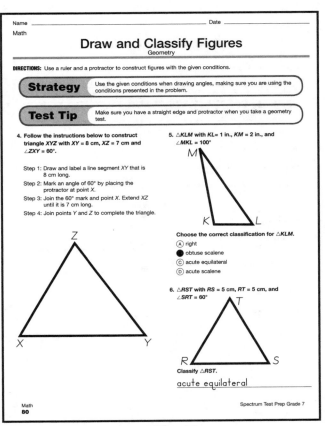

5. △KLM with KL = 1 in., KM = 2 in., and ∠MKL = 100°

Choose the correct classification for △KLM.

Ⓐ right
● obtuse scalene
Ⓒ acute equilateral
Ⓓ acute scalene

6. △RST with RS = 5 cm, RT = 5 cm, and ∠SRT = 60°

Classify △RST.

$\underline{acute\ equilateral}$

80

Page 81

Use Plane Sections
Geometry

DIRECTIONS: Choose or write the correct answer.

Strategy Use the characteristics of two- and three-dimensional figures to identify plane figures that are cross sections of three-dimensional figures.

1. Two right triangular pyramids with cross sections are shown below. Complete the sentences.

The shape of the base is a __rectangle__, so the cross section of a plane parallel to the base is a __rectangle__.

The shape of each side is a __triangle__, so the cross section of a plane perpendicular to the base is a __triangle__.

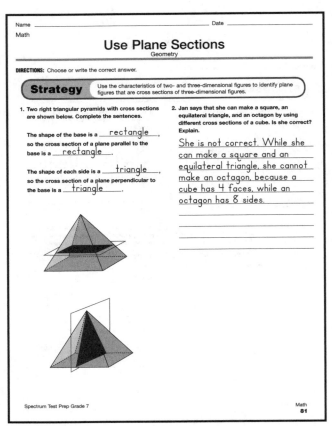

2. Jan says that she can make a square, an equilateral triangle, and an octagon by using different cross sections of a cube. Is she correct? Explain.

She is not correct. While she can make a square and an equilateral triangle, she cannot make an octagon, because a cube has 4 faces, while an octagon has 8 sides.

81

Page 82

Use Plane Sections
Geometry

DIRECTIONS: Choose or write the correct answer.

Strategy Use the attributes of shapes to identify a given plane within a shape.

Test Tip A plane is a flat section within a shape. A cross-section is a shape made when a plane cuts through a three-dimensional shape.

3. Name a cross section for each of these three-dimensional figures.

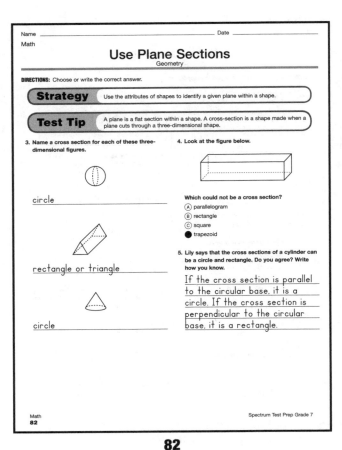

circle

rectangle or triangle

circle

4. Look at the figure below.

Which could not be a cross section?
- (A) parallelogram
- (B) rectangle
- (C) square
- ● trapezoid

5. Lily says that the cross sections of a cylinder can be a circle and rectangle. Do you agree? Write how you know.

If the cross section is parallel to the circular base, it is a circle. If the cross section is perpendicular to the circular base, it is a rectangle.

82

Page 83

Find Area of Circles
Geometry

DIRECTIONS: Choose or write the correct answer.

Strategy Use the formula $A = \pi r^2$ to find the area of a circle.

Test Tip Remember to include the correct units in the solution. The area of a figure is always in square units.

1. A flower garden in the shape of a circle has a diameter of 6 feet. What is the area of the garden? Use 3.14 for π.

The formula for the area of a circle is $A = \pi r^2$.

The diameter of the flower garden is 6 feet, so the radius is __3 feet__.

$A = \pi r^2 = 3.14 \times$ __3__$^2 = 3.14 \times$ __9__
= __28.26__ ft.²

2. Find the area of each circle. Round to the nearest tenth, if necessary. Use 3.14 for π.

a circle with r = 10 in.

__314 in.²__

a circle with r = 5 ft.

__78.5 ft.²__

a circle with d = 18 cm

__254.3 cm²__

3. A CD has a radius of 6 cm. What is the area of the CD? Use 3.14 for π.
- (A) 6.28 cm²
- (B) 59.18 cm²
- ● 113.04 cm²
- (D) 452.16 cm²

4. The base of a snare drum has an area of 153.86 in.² What is the diameter of the drum?
- (A) 7 in.
- ● 14 in.
- (C) 24.5 in.
- (D) 49 in.

83

Page 84

Find Circumference of Circles
Geometry

DIRECTIONS: Choose or write the correct answer.

Strategy Use the formulas $C = 2\pi r$ and $C = \pi d$ to find the circumference of a circle.

Test Tip Remember to include the correct units in the solution. Units for circumference are often inches, feet, centimeters, or meters.

1. A round swimming pool has a diameter of 18 feet. What is the circumference of the pool? Use 3.14 for π.

You are given the diameter, so use the formula for __$C = \pi d$__ to find the circumference.

The diameter of the pool is 18 feet, so the radius is __9 feet__.

$C = \pi d = 3.14 \times$ __18__ = __56.52__ feet

2. Find the circumference of each circle to the nearest hundredth. Use 3.14 for π.

circle with r = 4 m

__25.12 m__

circle with d = 7.5 ft.

__23.55 ft.__

circle with r = 13 in.

__81.64 in.__

3. Abby has an exercise wheel with an 11 in. diameter for her guinea pig. What is the circumference of the exercise wheel to the nearest whole number? Use 3.14 for π.
- (A) 17 in.
- ● 35 in.
- (C) 69 in.
- (D) 95 in.

4. Kai needs a new bicycle tire. His tire has a circumference of about 113.04 inches. What is the diameter of the tire?
- (A) 6 in.
- (B) 18 in.
- ● 36 in.
- (D) 72 in.

84

Use Angle Relationships
Geometry

DIRECTIONS: Use the figure below to answer the questions.

Strategy — Use facts about supplementary, complementary, vertical, and adjacent angles in a multi-step problem to write and solve simple equations for an unknown angle in a figure.

Test Tip — Add to determine the type of angle. Two supplementary angles added together equal 180°. Two complementary angles added together equal 90°. Vertical angles are equal; if you know the measure of one, you can find the measure of the other.

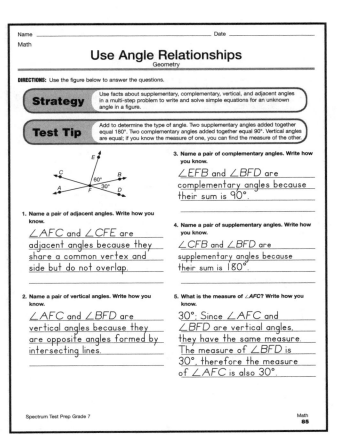

1. Name a pair of adjacent angles. Write how you know.

∠AFC and ∠CFE are adjacent angles because they share a common vertex and side but do not overlap.

2. Name a pair of vertical angles. Write how you know.

∠AFC and ∠BFD are vertical angles because they are opposite angles formed by intersecting lines.

3. Name a pair of complementary angles. Write how you know.

∠EFB and ∠BFD are complementary angles because their sum is 90°.

4. Name a pair of supplementary angles. Write how you know.

∠CFB and ∠BFD are supplementary angles because their sum is 180°.

5. What is the measure of ∠AFC? Write how you know.

30°; Since ∠AFC and ∠BFD are vertical angles, they have the same measure. The measure of ∠BFD is 30°, therefore the measure of ∠AFC is also 30°.

85

Use Angle Relationships
Geometry

DIRECTIONS: Use the figure to answer the questions.

Strategy — Read the word problems carefully to identify the measurements of angles you know and to make sure you know which angle measurement to solve for.

Test Tip — Remember that a full rotation of all angles forms a circle and equals 360°.

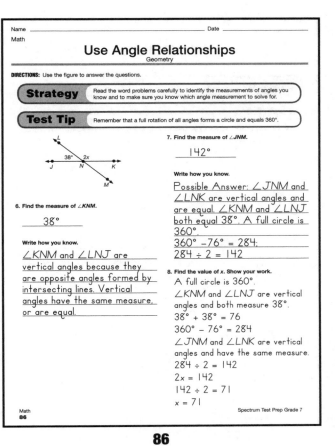

6. Find the measure of ∠KNM.

38°

Write how you know.

∠KNM and ∠LNJ are vertical angles because they are opposite angles formed by intersecting lines. Vertical angles have the same measure, or are equal.

7. Find the measure of ∠JNM.

142°

Write how you know.

Possible Answer: ∠JNM and ∠LNK are vertical angles and are equal. ∠KNM and ∠LNJ both equal 38°. A full circle is 360°.
360° −76° = 284;
284 ÷ 2 = 142

8. Find the value of x. Show your work.

A full circle is 360°.
∠KNM and ∠LNJ are vertical angles and both measure 38°.
38° + 38° = 76
360° − 76° = 284
∠JNM and ∠LNK are vertical angles and have the same measure.
284 ÷ 2 = 142
2x = 142
142 ÷ 2 = 71
x = 71

86

Use Angle Relationships
Geometry

Strategy — Identify whether the angle you are measuring or comparing is supplementary, complementary, or equal.

Test Tip — Study the definitions of geometric terms before your test.

DIRECTIONS: Use the figure below for problems 9 and 10.

DIRECTIONS: Use the figure below for problems 11 and 12.

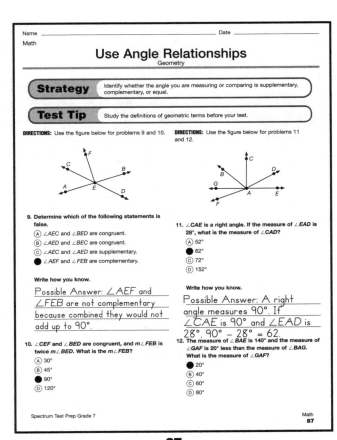

9. Determine which of the following statements is false.

Ⓐ ∠AEC and ∠BED are congruent.
Ⓑ ∠AED and ∠BEC are congruent.
Ⓒ ∠AEC and ∠AED are supplementary.
● ∠AEF and ∠FEB are complementary.

Write how you know.

Possible Answer: ∠AEF and ∠FEB are not complementary because combined they would not add up to 90°.

10. ∠CEF and ∠BED are congruent, and m∠FEB is twice m∠BED. What is the m∠FEB?

Ⓐ 30°
Ⓑ 45°
● 90°
Ⓓ 120°

11. ∠CAE is a right angle. If the measure of ∠EAD is 28°, what is the measure of ∠CAD?

Ⓐ 52°
● 62°
Ⓒ 72°
Ⓓ 152°

Write how you know.

Possible Answer: A right angle measures 90°. If ∠CAE is 90° and ∠EAD is 28°. 90° − 28° = 62.

12. The measure of ∠BAE is 140° and the measure of ∠GAF is 20° less than the measure of ∠BAG. What is the measure of ∠GAF?

● 20°
Ⓑ 40°
Ⓒ 60°
Ⓓ 80°

87

Find Volume
Geometry

DIRECTIONS: Use the figures to complete the statements.

Strategy — Use the formula for the volume of a prism. The volume V of a prism is the area of its base B times its height h. So, V = Bh

Test Tip — Read all parts of the question first.

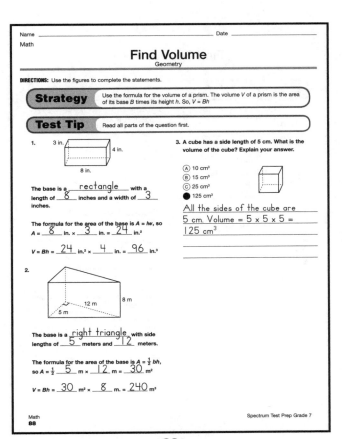

1.

The base is a **rectangle** with a length of **8** inches and a width of **3** inches.

The formula for the area of the base is A = lw, so
A = **8** in. × **3** in. = **24** in.²

V = Bh = **24** in.² × **4** in. = **96** in.³

2.

The base is a **right triangle** with side lengths of **5** meters and **12** meters.

The formula for the area of the base is A = ½ bh,
so A = ½ **5** m × **12** m = **30** m²

V = Bh = **30** m² × **8** m. = **240** m³

3. A cube has a side length of 5 cm. What is the volume of the cube? Explain your answer.

Ⓐ 10 cm³
Ⓑ 15 cm³
Ⓒ 25 cm³
● 125 cm³

All the sides of the cube are 5 cm. Volume = 5 × 5 × 5 = 125 cm³

88

Find Volume
Geometry

Strategy Use the formula for the volume of a cube. The volume *V* of a cube is the length *l* multiplied by its width *w* and height *h*. So, $V = l \times w \times h$

Test Tip Remember that the volume of a solid figure is always expressed in cubic units.

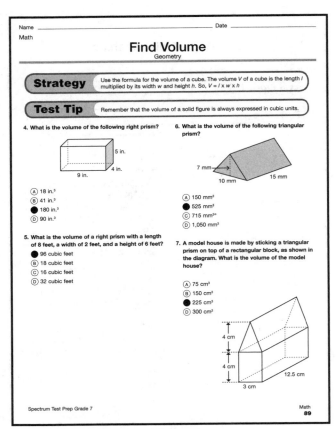

4. What is the volume of the following right prism?

- Ⓐ 18 in.³
- Ⓑ 41 in.³
- ● 180 in.³
- Ⓓ 90 in.³

5. What is the volume of a right prism with a length of 8 feet, a width of 2 feet, and a height of 6 feet?

- ● 96 cubic feet
- Ⓑ 18 cubic feet
- Ⓒ 16 cubic feet
- Ⓓ 32 cubic feet

6. What is the volume of the following triangular prism?

- Ⓐ 150 mm³
- ● 525 mm³
- Ⓒ 715 mm³°
- Ⓓ 1,050 mm³

7. A model house is made by sticking a triangular prism on top of a rectangular block, as shown in the diagram. What is the volume of the model house?

- Ⓐ 75 cm³
- Ⓑ 150 cm³
- ● 225 cm³
- Ⓓ 300 cm³

Find Surface Area
Geometry

DIRECTIONS: Use the figures below to answer the questions.

Strategy Use formulas for area and basic operations to find surface area. The surface area *SA* of a prism is the sum of the area of all its faces.

Test Tip Remember that the surface area of a solid figure is always expressed in square units.

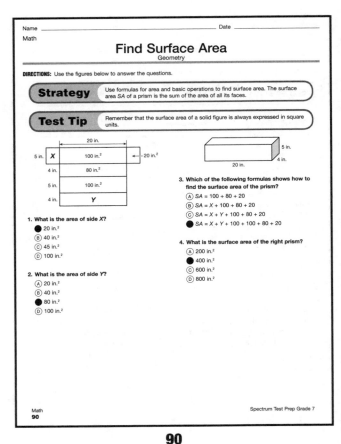

1. What is the area of side *X*?

- ● 20 in.²
- Ⓑ 40 in.²
- Ⓒ 45 in.²
- Ⓓ 100 in.²

2. What is the area of side *Y*?

- Ⓐ 20 in.²
- Ⓑ 40 in.²
- ● 80 in.²
- Ⓓ 100 in.²

3. Which of the following formulas shows how to find the surface area of the prism?

- Ⓐ $SA = 100 + 80 + 20$
- Ⓑ $SA = X + 100 + 80 + 20$
- Ⓒ $SA = X + Y + 100 + 80 + 20$
- ● $SA = X + Y + 100 + 100 + 80 + 20$

4. What is the surface area of the right prism?

- Ⓐ 200 in.²
- ● 400 in.²
- Ⓒ 600 in.²
- Ⓓ 800 in.²

Find Surface Area
Geometry

Strategy To find surface area, use or draw the shape involved, carefully labeling the measurements you know from the word problem.

5. A box in the shape of a cube has a side length of 8 in. What is the surface area of the box? Write how you know.

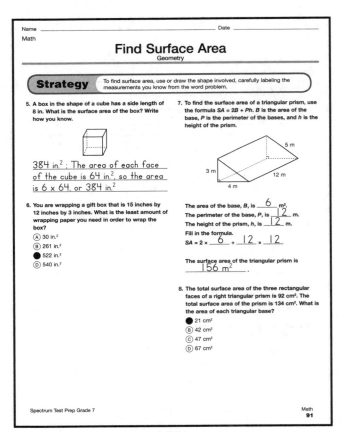

384 in.² ; The area of each face of the cube is 64 in.², so the area is 6 x 64, or 384 in.²

6. You are wrapping a gift box that is 15 inches by 12 inches by 3 inches. What is the least amount of wrapping paper you need in order to wrap the box?

- Ⓐ 30 in.²
- Ⓑ 261 in.²
- ● 522 in.²
- Ⓓ 540 in.²

7. To find the surface area of a triangular prism, use the formula $SA = 2B + Ph$. *B* is the area of the base, *P* is the perimeter of the bases, and *h* is the height of the prism.

The area of the base, *B*, is ___6___ m².
The perimeter of the base, *P*, is ___12___ m.
The height of the prism, *h*, is ___12___ m.
Fill in the formula.
$SA = 2 \times$ ___6___ $+$ ___12___ $\times$ ___12___

The surface area of the triangular prism is ___156 m²___.

8. The total surface area of the three rectangular faces of a right triangular prism is 92 cm². The total surface area of the prism is 134 cm². What is the area of each triangular base?

- ● 21 cm²
- Ⓑ 42 cm²
- Ⓒ 47 cm²
- Ⓓ 67 cm²

Understand Sampling
Statistics and Probability

DIRECTIONS: Explain your answers in complete sentences.

Strategy Gain information about a population by examining a sample of the population.

Test Tip Read each question carefully before deciding how to answer it.

1. In a random sample of 45 students in the school cafeteria, Alana found that 20 ordered a tuna wrap. If there are 405 students who eat the cafeteria lunch, how many will likely order a tuna wrap?

It is likely that about 180 students will order a tuna wrap.

2. Is the sample in question 1 a good sampling of the population? Explain.

This is a good sample because it is random and it is large enough to represent the entire population.

3. Why might you choose to use the sample survey rather than survey the entire population? Explain.

You might use a sample because it can be done more quickly than surveying the entire population.

4. Evan took a survey of favorite types of books from a random sample of 30 students. The books are to be sold in a bookstore at a school with 750 students. Should the sample be larger? Explain.

Yes, this sample should be larger than 4% of the population.

5. A pre-election poll predicted that a certain candidate for mayor would receive 30% of the vote. He actually received 70%. Was this poll useful? Explain.

No, the poll was not useful because it did not come close to predicting the actual outcome.

6. Give two reasons why the pre-election poll could have been so far off in question 5.

The poll could have been off because the sample was not random or the sample was not large enough.

7. A poll is being taken at a middle school to determine whether to change the school colors. Which would be the best place to find a sample of students who would be most representative of the entire student body?

- Ⓐ a math class
- ● the cafeteria
- Ⓒ the principal's office
- Ⓓ the music room

Use a Sample
Statistics and Probability

DIRECTIONS: Read the information. Then, answer the questions.

Strategy Use a random sample to make inferences about an entire population.

1. The data in the table was collected from two random samples of 100 students regarding students' school lunch preference. What inferences can be made based on the results?

	Hamburgers	Pizza	Hot Dogs	Total
Sample 1	20	64	16	100
Sample 2	14	68	18	100

It can be inferred that ___pizza___ is the first choice for school lunch.

Do students have much of a preference between hamburgers and hot dogs? Write how you know.

There is not much of a difference between hamburgers and hot dogs in either sample, so students don't seem to have much of a preference of hamburgers to hot dogs.

2. About how many slices of pizza should the school cafeteria prepare to serve 500 students?
   - Ⓐ 250
   - ● 330
   - Ⓒ 400
   - Ⓓ 500

3. Ben is ordering T-shirts for the school store. He surveyed and collected random samples of 100 students regarding student color preferences. Make at least two inferences based on the results.

	Yellow	White	Blue	Total
Sample 1	32	20	48	100
Sample 2	28	15	57	100

It can be inferred that blue is the first choice for T-shirt color. About half the students surveyed in each sample prefer blue. Yellow appears to be the second choice, and white the third choice.

4. Andrew is planning what to buy for his store downtown. He collected two random samples of 100 women regarding their preference. Choose all inferences that apply.

	Capris	Shorts	Pants	Total
Sample 1	59	16	25	100
Sample 2	49	23	28	100

- ● More than twice as many women prefer capris to shorts.
- Ⓑ More women prefer shorts than capris.
- ● Shorts and pants are about tied.
- ● Most women prefer capris.

93

Find the Mean, Median, and Mode
Statistics and Probability

Strategy Use the definitions of mean, median, and mode to compute them from a given data set.

Test Tip Always start by ordering the data from least to greatest.

DIRECTIONS: Use the following data set to answer questions 1–4.

8, 5, 8, 8, 10, 10, 13, 17, 17, 25, 20, 7, 9.

1. What is the mean of the data?
   - Ⓐ 8
   - Ⓑ 9.5
   - ● 12.25
   - Ⓓ 20

2. What is the median of the data?
   - Ⓐ 8
   - ● 9.5
   - Ⓒ 12.25
   - Ⓓ 20

3. What is the mode of the data?
   - ● 8
   - Ⓑ 9.5
   - Ⓒ 12.5
   - Ⓓ There is no mode.

DIRECTIONS: Use the following data set for questions 4–7.

The basketball attendance per game for the season was: 80, 100, 60, 120, 120, 100, 140.

4. What is the mean of the data?
   102.9

5. What is the median of the data?
   100

Test Tip Remember that there can be more than one mode for a data set.

6. What is the mode of the data?
   There are 2 modes: 100 and 120

7. Suppose there had been an additional basketball game in the season. Attendance at this game was 100. How would this affect the mean, mode, and median of the data set?

   The median would be unchanged, but the only mode would now be 100. The mean would become 102.5

94

Interpret Stem-and-Leaf Plots
Statistics and Probability

DIRECTIONS: Read the information. Then, answer the questions.

Strategy Use data to make and interpret a stem-and-leaf plot.

1. Becca recorded the heights (in inches) of the students in her art class in a stem-and-leaf plot.

4	8 9
5	0 3 7 7 9
6	1 2 2 4 6

Key: 5 | 3 means 53

How many students are in the art class?
12 students

How tall is the tallest person in the class?
66 inches

2. Elizabeth recorded her bowling scores in a stem-and-leaf plot.

9	7
10	0 2 7 8 9
11	1 3 3 4 6
12	0 5 8
13	2 4 6 9

Key: 12 | 5 means 125

What is Elizabeth's best score? *139*

What is the mode of Elizabeth's bowling scores?
113

Test Tip Remember to make a key when you make a stem-and-leaf plot.

3. Your class just took a math test. These are the scores: 97, 99, 81, 78, 73, 95, 63, 97, 64, 100, 85, 83, 85, 88, 79, 80, 93, 82, 85, and 71. Make a stem-and-leaf plot of the data.

6	3 4
7	1 3 8 9
8	0 1 2 3 5 5 5 8
9	3 5 7 7 9
10	0

Key: 6 | 3 means 63

What is the range of the test scores? Show your work.
The range is 37:
100 – 63 = 37

What is the mode of the test scores? *85*

What is the median of the test scores? Write how you know.
84: There are 20 test scores, so I found the average of the two middle scores, 83 and 85.

95

Interpret Box-and-Whisker Plots
Statistics and Probability

DIRECTIONS: The box-and-whisker plot shows the number of volunteer hours performed by the students in Ms. Becker's homeroom last year. Use the box-and-whisker plot to answer the questions.

Strategy Use box-and-whisker plots to interpret data sets.

Test Tip Box-and-whisker plots identify the lower and upper extremes, the first and third quartiles, and the median.

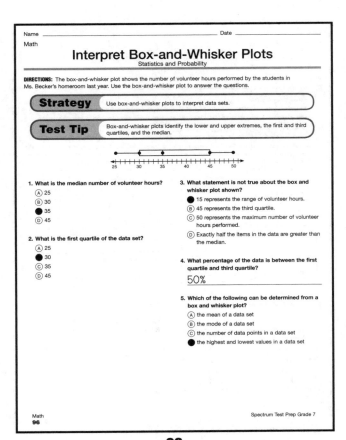

1. What is the median number of volunteer hours?
   - Ⓐ 25
   - Ⓑ 30
   - ● 35
   - Ⓓ 45

2. What is the first quartile of the data set?
   - Ⓐ 25
   - ● 30
   - Ⓒ 35
   - Ⓓ 45

3. What statement is not true about the box and whisker plot shown?
   - ● 15 represents the range of volunteer hours.
   - Ⓑ 45 represents the third quartile.
   - Ⓒ 50 represents the maximum number of volunteer hours performed.
   - Ⓓ Exactly half the items in the data are greater than the median.

4. What percentage of the data is between the first quartile and third quartile?
   50%

5. Which of the following can be determined from a box and whisker plot?
   - Ⓐ the mean of a data set
   - Ⓑ the mode of a data set
   - Ⓒ the number of data points in a data set
   - ● the highest and lowest values in a data set

96

Use Simple Probability
Statistics and Probability

DIRECTIONS: Read the information. Then, answer the questions.

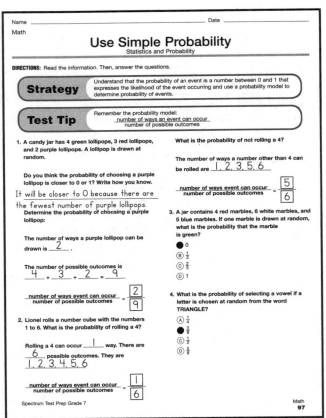

Strategy Understand that the probability of an event is a number between 0 and 1 that expresses the likelihood of the event occurring and use a probability model to determine probability of events.

Test Tip Remember the probability model:
$$\frac{\text{number of ways an event can occur}}{\text{number of possible outcomes}}$$

1. A candy jar has 4 green lollipops, 3 red lollipops, and 2 purple lollipops. A lollipop is drawn at random.

Do you think the probability of choosing a purple lollipop is closer to 0 or 1? Write how you know.

It will be closer to 0 because there are the fewest number of purple lollipops.

Determine the probability of choosing a purple lollipop:

The number of ways a purple lollipop can be drawn is __2__.

The number of possible outcomes is
__4__ + __3__ + __2__ = __9__

$$\frac{\text{number of ways event can occur}}{\text{number of possible outcomes}} = \frac{2}{9}$$

2. Lionel rolls a number cube with the numbers 1 to 6. What is the probability of rolling a 4?

Rolling a 4 can occur __1__ way. There are __6__ possible outcomes. They are
1, 2, 3, 4, 5, 6

$$\frac{\text{number of ways event can occur}}{\text{number of possible outcomes}} = \frac{1}{6}$$

What is the probability of not rolling a 4?

The number of ways a number other than 4 can be rolled are 1, 2, 3, 5, 6

$$\frac{\text{number of ways event can occur}}{\text{number of possible outcomes}} = \frac{5}{6}$$

3. A jar contains 4 red marbles, 6 white marbles, and 5 blue marbles. If one marble is drawn at random, what is the probability that the marble is green?

● A 0
B $\frac{1}{5}$
C $\frac{2}{5}$
D 1

4. What is the probability of selecting a vowel if a letter is chosen at random from the word TRIANGLE?

A $\frac{1}{4}$
● B $\frac{3}{8}$
C $\frac{1}{2}$
D $\frac{5}{8}$

Spectrum Test Prep Grade 7

Math
97

97

Use Experimental Probability
Statistics and Probability

DIRECTIONS: Read the information. Then, answer the questions.

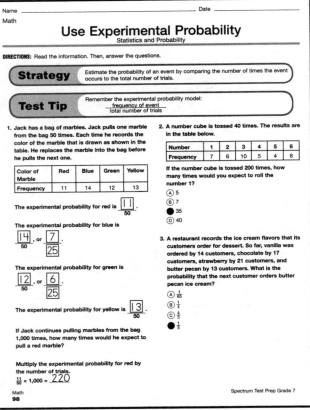

Strategy Estimate the probability of an event by comparing the number of times the event occurs to the total number of trials.

Test Tip Remember the experimental probability model:
$$\frac{\text{frequency of event}}{\text{total number of trials}}$$

1. Jack has a bag of marbles. Jack pulls one marble from the bag 50 times. Each time he records the color of the marble that is drawn as shown in the table. He replaces the marble into the bag before he pulls the next one.

Color of Marble	Red	Blue	Green	Yellow
Frequency	11	14	12	13

The experimental probability for red is $\frac{11}{50}$

The experimental probability for blue is $\frac{14}{50}$, or $\frac{7}{25}$

The experimental probability for green is $\frac{12}{50}$, or $\frac{6}{25}$

The experimental probability for yellow is $\frac{13}{50}$

If Jack continues pulling marbles from the bag 1,000 times, how many times would he expect to pull a red marble?

Multiply the experimental probability for red by the number of trials.
$\frac{11}{50} \times 1,000 = $ __220__

2. A number cube is tossed 40 times. The results are in the table below.

Number	1	2	3	4	5	6
Frequency	7	6	10	5	4	8

If the number cube is tossed 200 times, how many times would you expect to roll the number 1?

A 5
B 7
● 35
D 40

3. A restaurant records the ice cream flavors that its customers order for dessert. So far, vanilla was ordered by 14 customers, chocolate by 17 customers, strawberry by 21 customers, and butter pecan by 13 customers. What is the probability that the next customer orders butter pecan ice cream?

A $\frac{1}{65}$
B $\frac{1}{4}$
C $\frac{4}{5}$
● $\frac{1}{5}$

Math
98

Spectrum Test Prep Grade 7

98

Use Compound Probability
Statistics and Probability

DIRECTIONS: Read the information. Then, answer the questions.

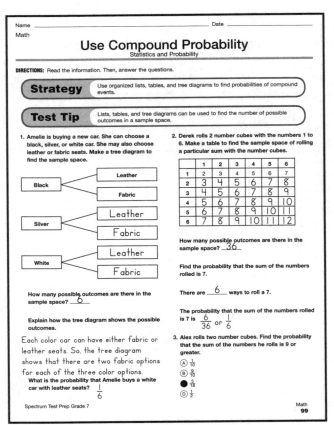

Strategy Use organized lists, tables, and tree diagrams to find probabilities of compound events.

Test Tip Lists, tables, and tree diagrams can be used to find the number of possible outcomes in a sample space.

1. Amelie is buying a new car. She can choose a black, silver, or white car. She may also choose leather or fabric seats. Make a tree diagram to find the sample space.

Black — Leather / Fabric
Silver — Leather / Fabric
White — Leather / Fabric

How many possible outcomes are there in the sample space? __6__

Explain how the tree diagram shows the possible outcomes.

Each color car can have either fabric or leather seats. So, the tree diagram shows that there are two fabric options for each of the three color options.

What is the probability that Amelie buys a white car with leather seats? $\frac{1}{6}$

2. Derek rolls 2 number cubes with the numbers 1 to 6. Make a table to find the sample space of rolling a particular sum with the number cubes.

	1	2	3	4	5	6
1	2	3	4	5	6	7
2	3	4	5	6	7	8
3	4	5	6	7	8	9
4	5	6	7	8	9	10
5	6	7	8	9	10	11
6	7	8	9	10	11	12

How many possible outcomes are there in the sample space? __36__

Find the probability that the sum of the numbers rolled is 7.

There are __6__ ways to roll a 7.

The probability that the sum of the numbers rolled is 7 is $\frac{6}{36}$ or $\frac{1}{6}$.

3. Alex rolls two number cubes. Find the probability that the sum of the numbers he rolls is 9 or greater.

A $\frac{1}{10}$
B $\frac{9}{10}$
● $\frac{5}{18}$
D $\frac{1}{2}$

Spectrum Test Prep Grade 7

Math
99

99

Strategy Review

DIRECTIONS: Answer the questions.

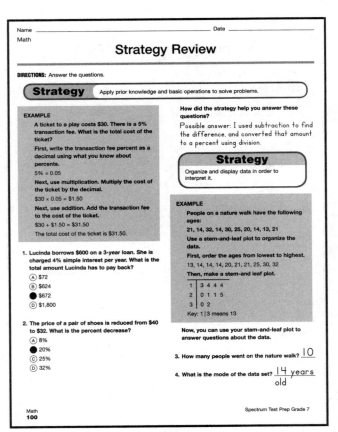

Strategy Apply prior knowledge and basic operations to solve problems.

EXAMPLE
A ticket to a play costs $30. There is a 5% transaction fee. What is the total cost of the ticket?
First, write the transaction fee percent as a decimal using what you know about percents.
5% = 0.05
Next, use multiplication. Multiply the cost of the ticket by the decimal.
$30 × 0.05 = $1.50
Next, use addition. Add the transaction fee to the cost of the ticket.
$30 + $1.50 = $31.50
The total cost of the ticket is $31.50.

1. Lucinda borrows $600 on a 3-year loan. She is charged 4% simple interest per year. What is the total amount Lucinda has to pay back?
A $72
B $624
● $672
D $1,800

2. The price of a pair of shoes is reduced from $40 to $32. What is the percent decrease?
A 8%
● 20%
C 25%
D 32%

How did the strategy help you answer these questions?
Possible answer: I used subtraction to find the difference, and converted that amount to a percent using division.

Strategy Organize and display data in order to interpret it.

EXAMPLE
People on a nature walk have the following ages:
21, 14, 32, 14, 30, 25, 20, 14, 13, 21
Use a stem-and-leaf plot to organize the data.
First, order the ages from lowest to highest.
13, 14, 14, 14, 20, 21, 21, 25, 30, 32
Then, make a stem-and leaf plot.

1	3 4 4 4
2	0 1 1 5
3	0 2

Key: 1 | 3 means 13

Now, you can use your stem-and-leaf plot to answer questions about the data.

3. How many people went on the nature walk? __10__

4. What is the mode of the data set? __14 years old__

Math
100

Spectrum Test Prep Grade 7

100

Spectrum Test Prep Grade 7

Strategy Review

Strategy Look for key words in word problems that help you know which operation to use.

EXAMPLE

A game show contestant has 50 points. He answers a question correctly to win 15 points. Then, he answers 3 questions incorrectly and loses 25 points each time. What is the contestant's final score?

First, identify key words that tell you what operations to use.

The words "win 15 points" suggest addition.

The words "loses 25 points" suggest subtraction.

The words "each time" suggest multiplication.

Then, write an expression to represent the situation.

$50 + 15 - 3(25)$

Perform all multiplications and divisions, working from left to right. Separate each calculation as needed.

$50 + 15 - 3(25) = 50 + 15 - 75$

Continue performing operations working from left to right.

$50 + 15 - 75 = 65 - 75 = -10$

The contestant's final score is –10.

Strategy Use drawings, graphs, or number lines to understand and solve a problem.

EXAMPLE

The temperature in Tannerville is –4°F. The temperature in Albion is 3 degrees less. What is the temperature in Albion?

First, draw a number line and plot the temperature in Tannerville.

−7 −6 −5 −4 −3 −2 −1 0

Then, move 3 tick marks to the left to show that the temperature in Albion is 3 degrees less.

−7 −6 −5 −4 −3 −2 −1 0

The temperature in Albion is –7°F.

2. A diver at 67 feet below the surface rises 10 feet. She then rises another 22 feet. She then moves 10 feet deeper. How many feet below the water's surface is the diver now? Make a drawing that helps you solve the problem.

a drawing showing the given levels or a number line

1. In a football game in the first 5 plays, the Falcons gained 2 yards, lost 8 yards, gained 3 yards, lost 2 yards, and then lost 5 yards. What was the average gain or loss for the 5 plays?

(A) 4 yards
● –2 yards
(C) –5 yards
(D) –10 yards

101

Strategy Review

Strategy Write and solve an equation to solve a real-world problem.

EXAMPLE

Julia spent $38 for shoes. This was $14 more than twice the cost of the belt she bought. How much was the belt?

First, write an equation that represents the situation or the problem.

Use b to represent the cost of the belt. The shoes cost $14 more than twice the cost of the belt.

So, the equation is
$38 = 14 + 2b$, or $2b + 14 = 38$.

Next, solve the equation for b.

$2b + 14 = 38$
$2b + 14 - 14 = 38 - 14$
Subtract 14 from both sides of the equation.
$2b = 24$
$\frac{2b}{2} = \frac{24}{2}$
Divide both sides by 2.
$b = 12$
The belt cost $12.

Strategy Read word problems carefully to identify the given information and what you are being asked to find.

EXAMPLE

Tanya collects coins and stamps. She traded 3 less than one-half of her coins for some stamps. She has 17 coins now. She wants to collect 17 more by the end of the month. How many coins did Tanya start with?

What is the given information?
Tanya traded 3 less than one-half of her coins. She has 17 coins now. She wants to collect 17 more.

What are you being asked to find?
the number of coins she started with

1. Pedro works 7 hours less than twice the number of hours that Gina works each week. If Pedro works 35 hours, how many hours does Gina work?

(A) 70
(B) 28
● 21
(D) 14

2. Bryan's mother is 5 years younger than 4 times the age of Bryan. If Bryan's mother is 39, how old is Bryan?

(A) 7
(B) $8\frac{1}{2}$
● 11
(D) $11\frac{1}{2}$

3. 159 students and teachers went on a field trip to the zoo. They left at 9:00 A.M. There were 3 buses and a van. All were filled. 6 students had to travel in a van. How many people were in each bus?

What is the given information?

159 students and teachers went on buses. They left at 9:00 A.M. There were 3 full buses and 6 students went in a van.

What are you being asked to find?

how many people were in each bus

Is any of the given information extra, or not needed?

Yes, we do not need to know what time they left.

102

Strategy Review

Strategy Use rules, properties, or formulas to solve problems.

EXAMPLE

An online store uses shipping cartons that are 14 in. by 12 in. by 6 in. Use the formula for volume, $V = Bh$, to find the volume of the carton.

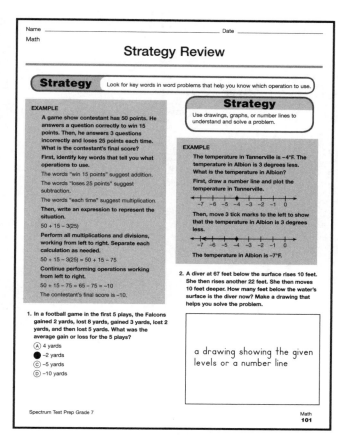

First, write the formula for the volume of a right rectangular prism.

$V = Bh$

Find the area of the base.

The base is a rectangle.
$A = lw = 12 \times 8 = 96$ in.²

Use the volume formula.

$V = Bh = 96 \times 6 = 576$ in.³

The volume of the carton is 576 in.³

1. Find the surface area of the shipping carton in the example.

648 in.³

2. Garrett is making new seat cushions for his dining room chairs. The cushion is in the shape of a rectangular prism whose dimensions are 15 in. by 18 in. by 2 in. He is stuffing the cushions with foam. How much foam does he need for one cushion?

(A) 336 in.³
● 540 in.³
(C) 672 in.³
(D) 1,080 in.³

3. Garrett is covering each seat cushion with material. How much material is needed for one cushion?

(A) 336 in.²
(B) 540 in.²
● 672 in.²
(D) 1,080 in.²

103